Debbie's Story

A JOURNEY TO HEALING

by

Debbie Neville
as told to
Jenny Harrison

SOUTHERN
BOOK PUBLISHERS

On wings I

acquired through suffering,

I will soar

Gustav Mahler

ISBN 1 86812 693 5

First edition, first impression 1997

Published by
Southern Book Publishers (Pty) Ltd
PO Box 3103, Halfway House 1685

Cover design by Alix Gracie
Set in 8.8/11pt Stone Serif
Reproduction by cmyk pre-press, Cape Town
Printed and bound by Colorgraphic, Pinetown

Debbie's Story

A JOURNEY TO HEALING

This book is dedicated to

The women who have had the courage to heal

The women who still have the pathway
of healing before them

The women who came to me in pain
and taught me how to listen

and especially

TO RUTH

my best friend
whose unconditional and consistent love
and encouragement over all the years
has never changed.

Thank you for teaching me
how to love and for giving your life
in service to God

My thanks to

- my husband, Mike, for understanding and loving me through the healing
- my children, Bernadette, Ryan and Robyn, for their patience and love and for allowing me to learn as I go along
- Emma for allowing me the freedom and safety to find myself

Debbie

My thanks to

- my husband, Howard, who knew all along that I could
- my children in the United States, England, New Zealand and South Africa who kept the enthusiasm at boiling point
- Dr Bernard Levinson who, like King Wenceslas, made footprints in the snow for me to follow

Jenny

We would also like
to thank the staff of Southern Books
in Midrand for their enthusiasm and support for this project.
In particular our thanks go to Louise Grantham and
Basil van Rooyen whose passionate belief in this book
made everything possible.

FOREWORD

Who are the child molesters? In our culture, they are usually male. Some 15 per cent of these individuals are totally unaware of the enormity of their actions. These are the feeble-minded and the psychotic, who are neither in control nor able to understand what they are doing. These incidents occur most commonly in institutions and rarely reach the courts.

Another 15 per cent are psychopathic. These are the dangerous child molesters. It is from this group that child pornography begins and spreads. The sexually molested child can be badly injured or killed. The word paedophile conjures up such an individual. These are the cases that hit the headlines in newspapers all over the world. The entire problem of paedophilia or child molesting is deeply coloured by this group. It is often difficult to unravel their brutal destructive psyche and understand this horrific need. The innocence and trust of children instantaneously brings out a powerful protective and caring need in all of us. It is completely bewildering to find individuals who wish to harm children.

The remaining 70 per cent of child molesters are normal men. They may be related to the child. Sometimes, sadly, closely related. They are always known to the child. A neighbour, the father of a friend, a school teacher. The sexual molesting is always committed under the guise of love. The grandfather who bothers his grandchild and spends too much time and care cleaning the genitalia. In some ways, this is the most damaging to the child. Love is contaminated. There is a betrayal. In the first two groups there is no question about immediately reporting the incident. There is terror and open aggression. The child runs for help. In the last large group, the child is trapped. Disclosure will either not be believed or will create havoc in the family. The trauma is there in the silence. The repressed awareness and the endless warping of our sexuality as an adult.

Is this response inevitable and for all time cemented? This is the importance of Debbie Neville's book. Healing is possible. A great deal of honest, patient love can reverse the fear and pain of such a childhood trauma.

Debbie allows us an intimate view of her lost, desperate parents. The demons that drive them, and at each stage an amazingly honest sharing of her innermost feelings. I was deeply moved by her heroic act of sharing this with us.

Not only will this book open the eyes of any individual unaware of the sad plight of children caught in these circumstances, but more importantly it will echo secret memories in so many men and women. They will know they are not alone.

My hope is that this book will give them the courage to hold on — to know that love, real love, can finally anchor them in another kind of world.

Dr Bernard Levinson

Prologue

Debbie Neville is a survivor of childhood sexual abuse. Out of the anguish of those youthful years has grown a peaceful woman. With healing has come a desire to help those who have suffered abuse as children and those who are still suffering abuse of one kind or another. Through private counselling and public debate it became obvious to Debbie that there are scores of men and women who are afraid to open their personal Pandora's boxes and she realised that one way to reach these people would be through self-disclosure.* This book, therefore, is not only a chronicle of a lost childhood but also the story of how one woman was able to confront her own demons and then to turn those demons into angels.

Debbie and I first met in 1992 when we worked as lay counsellors for Life Line on the West Rand. I was involved in the Rape Crisis Team and Debbie, because of her experiences, had been appointed as one of the trainers and a special advisor to the team. When Debbie and I first met there was an immediate rapport, each of us aware that we would work together, although the actual project had not yet been conceived. I found her open and honest not only about her weaknesses (which most of us can manage without much effort) but also her strengths (a more rare quality). Most of all I discovered in Debbie a uniquely compassionate human being with the ability to access the deepest, most anguished parts of the human psyche and through a gentle and loving touch to be midwife to a process of healing in others. Truly a gift from the depths.

I don't believe in coincidence. For me a coincidence is only one of God's unsigned miracles. With miracles, signed or unsigned, there is always divine intention and design. Meeting Debbie Neville was part of my par-

---

*Experts now estimate that one girl out of every four will be sexually molested in some way before the age of twenty ... boys seem to be abused sexually with the same frequency as that of girls — one out of four.
Sexual abuse of children in South Africa, by Grant Robertson, p. 1.

ticular spiritual journey and for Debbie our friendship and the resultant book has become the continuum of her personal path of healing.

From the time that I could hold a pen, I dreamed of being a writer. In those early days I was probably not too sure what being a "writer" meant, except that I was positive I would acquire fame and fortune and that those people who had ignored and humiliated me as a child would suddenly be grovelling at my feet. One personality trait, however, held me back. I was, and am, a dedicated procrastinator. The only time I do anything is when not doing it is life threatening. If I had tried to be a writer, with all the ego motives securely in place and before I was spiritually and emotionally ready, if I had written and failed, had tried again and probably failed, this book would never have been written. I would not have had the courage to tackle it and Debbie might not have felt that she was capable of doing it alone. Was procrastination a gift rather than a flaw — a gift that embraced and held me in readiness until my own growing spiritual awareness and wisdom were ready for the role of creative amanuensis to Debbie Neville? Was I then "released" to act in a way that was free of selfish and ego-centred motives? Was it only then that I could write a book of this importance, in the name of another and only for love and the desire to serve? I wonder. Part of my future spiritual quest will include looking at other flaws and failures and seeing them as gifts of the spirit cajoling and encouraging me forward. In this Debbie and I have walked similar paths, for she too has had to look at her life and see through the trauma to the gift within.

When Debbie and I first became friends she was counselling prostitutes and drug addicts in Johannesburg's notorious Hillbrow district. I remember the two of us sitting in the Life Line counselling room, where I questioned her on her experiences with these sad people. Something I said must have triggered an idea, for she looked at me thoughtfully, as if weighing me up. Some while later we had lunch together.

"Jen," she said, "I want to run something by you."

"Sure, what's the problem?"

"I want to write a book about my life and I need your help." And that was the start.

Debbie had come to the place in her life where she knew that the only way to be free of the past was to turn around and face it, to acknowledge the horrific events and to outstare the darkness from which they came. In doing so she would be able to show other survivors that there is life after abuse and rape and that life can be good.

The project became more complex in the weeks that followed. The journey we took together became a courageous demonstration of the tenacity of the human spirit, its will to regenerate and flourish. There was also a brave commitment on Debbie's part to open her life to the scrutiny of others in order to prove that healing is possible after the murderous storms suffered by the abused child. She realised that those demons could not survive the light of day and that the best way to bring them into the light and thereby divest them of their power was by sharing them with others.

I didn't realise in the beginning what incredible courage this was going to take or how this was to be the expiation of much of her pain. The journey proved to be painful and frightening for both of us. In remembering, Debbie began to re-experience the past. It was as if putting the events on paper had the power to validate them. Suddenly the horror was real again. Her nightmares returned and many of her old fears resurfaced. As a lay counsellor I did not have the experience to know what questions to ask and was often at a loss in the face of her early despair. There were times when I wondered whether we were stirring dragons which were better left sleeping — until I realised the cathartic value of full revelation. Often I would have to walk away from my computer, unable to stomach the depth of cruelty and abasement, sickened by the destruction of trust and deeply saddened by the loss of a precious childhood. It took a long time before I was able to see the adults in Debbie's childhood with anything but abhorrence.

Debbie had lived a life of chaos and it took patience and understanding for us to make coherent sense of what had happened. As we sat week after week working with the material I began to feel much like a surgeon, gently but painfully excising secrets that had lain festering for thirty years, experiences that Debbie had not revealed to anyone.

I valued the trust she had in me as, in some way, it reclaimed a part of myself that was worthy of such trust. Debbie had travelled much of this path alone and then she chose to trust me as a partner in her quest for healing. This is, for me, the ultimate privilege.

So, the book is done and the ghosts are largely at rest. Debbie has redeemed the past and turned it to glorious account, and this is her story.

Jenny Harrison
Kloofendal
February 1996

Chapter 1

Great Britain Street in Kenilworth, to the south of Johannesburg, is wide and almost treeless, humped in the middle so that the summer rains drain into the gutters on either side. Walking west along its cracked and lumpy pavement one passes Marine Court, crouched defiantly facing the elderly road. On either side of Marine Court and all along Great Britain Street the houses squat four-square in gardens so small they look like well-corseted, breathless old ladies, bulging through flimsy respectability. Then, as now, dirty-faced children played in the street, hopscotch squares chalked haphazardly on the cracked paving stones, frayed skipping ropes winding through the air, little girls who were never children sat with their bare feet in the gutters talking to dolls whose faces had long since been kissed clear of recognisable features. In the houses mothers, fathers and extended families fought, drank, gossiped and copulated behind grubby net curtains.

Most of the homes in Great Britain Street were built for the whey-faced, weary men who returned from the Second World War. They were, and still are, artisan's houses, honey brick like Marine Court, or cream painted plaster. Dull, ordinary houses, enclosing for the most part dull, ordinary lives.

Before the Second World War my grandmother, May, had been married to Warren Nicholls. It was an uneasy marriage, with Warren often using his fists and boots to bring his version of order into the home. When war broke out Warren enlisted in the South African Army and left May with two teenage rapscallions to control while he marched away — no doubt with a sense of relief. Douglas and Basil were in their early teens when Warren joined up and both were wild and difficult children. Like their father, they were easily angered and fast with their fists and boots. Warren's fierce and uncontrollable temper, fired by alcohol, and a tendency to hit first and ask questions much later, if at all, had been a dark inspiration to his wayward boys.

One incident which May vividly remembered was the day Warren came home with two pairs of small boxing gloves. He dragged the little boys from their play, forced their hands into the gloves and pushed them out into the back yard. Then he stood by smiling sardonically as the boys feebly punched at one another until they drew blood. This became a Saturday afternoon ritual, the boys pitted one against the other and Warren insisting that they "slug it out like men". If one cried Warren would fetch the leather belt that hung ominously from a hook on the back porch and beat both of them until red welts stood up on their legs. May watched from behind the kitchen curtains, suffering with each blow as the two little boys punched at each other and snivelled into their gloves. There was little she could do, for she was as afraid of Warren as they were. She supposed that this was a lesson the boys needed to learn to become men, to be unafraid and to be able to hold their own one day. Her boys would not be sissies or crybabies, she promised herself, but it was hard to watch them being beaten and ridiculed.

While still in their teens both boys had begun to drink and smoke and "act up". The Nicholls boys developed a reputation in the area for their wild ways and their drinking bouts. They were bullies and hellhounds, often in trouble with the law and their neighbours. It was at this time that their mother set a pattern that was to last all of their days. May blindly adored her boys and saw no wrong in either of them, whatever the neighbours and the law said. Whenever they were in trouble she convinced herself and the boys that someone else was at fault. And so it happened that whatever the problem, whether at school, with the neighbours and finally with the police, May would rush to her boys' aid and "rescue" them. It was never their fault; they were blameless, according to May, and the accountability was always apportioned to someone or something else. Back home, she would use their misdemeanours as weapons against them; emotional manipulation became her forte and her style of mothering.

During the war May worked as an ambulance driver for the Johannesburg Municipality and it was there that she met Andy Reynolds. Andy was a big lumbering sort of man, quiet with pale grey eyes. He saw much and said little. It was probably May's vivacious personality, so different from his own, that captivated him, although he knew that she had a husband "up north".

Andy remembered the day in 1942 when the government letter came for May. He had seen other women crying quietly when a letter like that arrived: *It is with regret that we have to inform you that your husband, Trooper Warren Nicholls, died in action on 18 June in Libya.*

Not long after this May agreed to marry Andy. For both of them it was the second time round and the romance transient and practical. Theirs was a brief courtship and a registry office marriage. There was no honeymoon, their important work as ambulance drivers didn't allow for such frivolities. And then there were May's two boys. They couldn't be left. Without much fuss May and Andy began their lives together with Douglas and Basil in

Marine Court.

The family were no sooner settled when Douglas, the eldest, swaggered into the lounge wearing the khaki uniform of the South African Army. At sixteen Basil was too young to join up, but he must have been dazzled by his older brother's swagger and style, because a few months later he ran away from home and joined the Navy.

May was frantic. "There's not much I can do about Doug. He's over age. But Basil, the fool, does he really think he's going to get away with this?" she fretted.

"Leave him, May. It's probably the best thing that could happen. Make a man of him," Andy said.

"Leave him? That'll be the day. He's my boy. I can't just let him go like that."

"What'll you do?" Andy was getting used to the firm control that May had over her family.

"I've already done it, lover boy. I wrote to Ouma Smuts and told her the story. She'll find him for me. Just you watch."

Not many weeks later a letter arrived from the formidable wife of the Prime Minister of South Africa, Jan Smuts. "Ouma" Smuts had traced Basil and told May where he was and that he was well. May showed the letter to her fellow workers at the ambulance depot and from that moment no one ever doubted that May Reynolds was a woman to be reckoned with.

Basil served in the Navy until the end of the war, frequently in trouble, frequently in detention barracks; never ever, according to May, at fault. In 1945 he and Douglas returned to Great Britain Street to resume their troubled lives. By now Andy and May had bought the house at No. 38 and although it was small both Douglas and Basil saw this home as their cornucopia from which all sustenance flowed.

May had a fine contralto voice and she loved to sing. In her youth and before the war she sang only in church and at private parties. During the war years May began to find herself in popular demand and would sing whenever and wherever she was asked. Soon after the war she began to sing professionally and soon had a small coterie of fans. Standing on a small stage in front of a microphone her powerful voice would erupt from deep down in her solid frame and her face radiate with a sense of fun that always entranced the audience. Now that she was happily married to Andy and her boys were home May had something to sing about. In peace time there were always charity shows or pub evenings where a strong raunchy voice like hers would be in demand. May loved the old Vera Lynn favourites and knew that they would always be welcomed by her audience. She sang them loudly and somehow managed to infuse them with a kind of sexual ambivalence which would have shocked Miss Lynn but obviously thrilled her audiences. When May got up on stage to sing her flat, almost Slavic features would light up and one could almost believe that she was beautiful.

Singing soon became May's life and invitations to sing at various events began to stream in. On Fridays and Saturdays she would be somewhere in Johannesburg, singing her heart out. Once they were married Andy stayed at home when May was out singing. He would not admit to anyone that he was slightly deaf and I don't think he particularly liked the camp backstage atmosphere of the places where his wife worked. Instead he would stay at home and make sure that when May returned she would find the garage doors open and a strong cup of coffee waiting in the kitchen.

May's career began to bring in a second income. This became essential as both boys went back to their old ways and were in frequent trouble with the police. Bail money was often needed, together with money for court appearances and fines. Then when May and Andy were landed with my sister Jenny and then with me to look after, every penny became important.

Not long after the end of the war Douglas met Madge and brought her home for May's approval. Madge was a friendly young girl with dark curly hair and a ready smile. Douglas desperately wanted to marry her and when she hesitated he raged and fumed and finally threatened to commit suicide. Years later Madge told me that she had felt trapped by his passionate pleas and morose threats and there had seemed to be little alternative to this emotional blackmail but to marry him. Then Basil brought Myra Best, my mother, home. Myra lived a few streets away but "everyone" in Kenilworth knew that her parents were violent and chronic alcoholics. These people were "beneath" May and her family, and Basil felt the lash of her furious tongue when he first admitted to visiting Myra.

May's disapproval was ominous. She did not want her boys marrying. She probably realised that if they did she would no longer have any control over them, and May was fanatically possessive of her boys. She needed to be in charge, needed to manipulate, and hated the thought that the boys were looking elsewhere for love and attention. But neither son obeyed her in matters of the heart. Douglas married his Madge and Basil married Myra soon after.

Both these girls seem to have married out of a sense of fear rather than genuine love and it wasn't long before both regretted their choice. Now, the boys had new boxing partners and both girls were subjected to severe beatings, probably before their weddings and certainly from the outset of their marriages.

Neither Douglas nor my father was able to hold a job for long. They drank and fought their way out of favour with one employer after another. When they were out of a job they inevitably found their way, together with their wives and burgeoning families, to May's front door.

May was always "there" for her boys. She would take them in, feed them, manipulate them and their families and "prove" to herself and anyone else within earshot that "her boys" needed her and not those stupid little girls they had married. It was only a mother who could make things right for them. It was only a mother who would pay the bail money and it was a mother who took responsibility for them whenever they got into trouble. May made sure, however, that the boys and their wives knew that they "owed her big time" and that pay-back time would inevitably come.

Finally Douglas decided that he needed to straighten out his life. He needed to be away from his mother and her obsessiveness. I think he began to understand that by taking responsibility away from him, his mother was actually preventing him from growing to full adulthood. He began to recognise that May was warped in her ideas of parenting and that this twist in her nature was becoming increasingly dangerous for his wife and three children.

In 1954 Douglas left Madge and the children with her parents and went to Durban to find a new job and home. One evening he phoned her to say that he had found the work he was looking for and a place to live, and he asked her to bring the children down to Durban as soon as possible. They would be starting again.

Madge was overjoyed. Now she would be away from May and the emotional machinations that filled life with such tension. Things were going to be all right at last. The following night she got a phone call from the police in Durban to say that Douglas was dead. He had been stabbed to death in a fight.

On hearing the news May collapsed. Her child was dead and nothing would ever be the same again. When she recovered from the initial shock she packed a small bag, took my sister Jenny with her and flew down to Durban to identify his body. When I asked Madge why she was not the one to identify her husband's body the reply was interesting.

"Debbie, you don't understand," she said. "May never acknowledged me as Doug's wife. I was an intruder and a temporary one at that. When Doug died all her maternal instincts kicked in and she just took over. She simply would not allow me to go to Durban to identify the body of my husband."

Madge had wanted Douglas buried in Durban but May insisted that his body be brought back to Johannesburg. Madge consulted a lawyer who advised her to let May do whatever she wanted, as long as she paid for it herself. Douglas was buried in Johannesburg two weeks later.

It was years later that my aunt Madge told me this story. It was only then that I began to see how important it was for my grandmother to have dominion over the members of her family and to recognise her careless-ness, or perhaps more kindly, her misunderstanding of the dynamics of a loving family, when it came to their true well-being and happiness. As a child I was so subject to her sovereignty over us that I took it for granted that this was the way things were done in all families. It was only much later as a teenager that I began to question this kind of arbitrary authority.

Looking back now, I think May did love her family, but somehow and somewhere along the way she had lost the ability to love unconditionally and, more importantly, lost the ability to know when to let go of her chil-dren for their own sakes. At various times both Basil and Douglas tried hard to break away from their mother, but neither ever managed it. They would go away with their families and then suddenly everything would come crashing down and they would be inexorably drawn back to May's web. My mother, Myra, and my father, Basil, and their two children would soon become the next tragic victims of her perverted love.

Chapter 2

As a small child I never knew my mother, Myra, for she abandoned me when I was six months old. Those parts of her life that I have been able to piece together show a tragically insecure figure who lived a lifetime of remorse and longing for the husband and children that she left. I suppose it was inevitable that Myra would become an alcoholic. She drank with my father to win his approval when she was with him. Later, when she had left him, she drank to forget: and in drinking it seemed that she remembered all the more vividly.

Myra Best was born in 1923. Because the Bests were alcoholic and violent I would guess that Myra's childhood was very similar to mine, filled with misery and moments of sheer terror. There is no one left who can tell me how she met my father, but they were married when she was about twenty and within a year my sister Jenny was born in the small flat in Malvern where Myra and Basil had set up home. Basil worked sporadically and Myra's expensive tastes soon landed the two in deep financial waters. May, of course, was always on hand with money, advice and admonitions and it is probably safe to say that Myra started drinking heavily and consistently at this time not only to keep Basil company but also in order to be able to face her mother-in-law's intrusive presence.

The emotional tension between the two women hung like a thundercloud and Basil continued dealing with it in his old way, drinking, brawling, being arrested and having to be bailed out of trouble. Now, however, there was a wife and a baby to drag along when he landed on May's doorstep, out of work, needing a square meal or to be helped out of some scrape or another. Basil bitterly resented his mother's power and his own weakness and May, in turn, resented Myra.

It is evident that right from the start of their marriage my grandmother did everything she could to cause a rift between my mother and father. I believe now that May was almost incestuously jealous of Myra. Here was a young slip of a girl who had the temerity to "steal" away her boy — and May never let go of a grudge. Whether she was consciously determined to end Basil's marriage to Myra Best or not I cannot be sure, but the end result was the same. Granny May never tired of telling me, with vindictive triumph, how she brought her boy home where he "belonged". It seems that the intense competition for Basil's affection together with the constant drunkenness and violence of her household finally wore Myra out and when Jenny was eight years old Myra divorced Basil and left Johannesburg.

May Reynolds had won.

Basil, once again, landed on her doorstep, tearfully drunk, with Jenny in tow. He could not look after this small bewildered child. He could not even look after himself. And so Jenny and Basil moved in with May and the ever-patient Andy. With no ties and no responsibilities and a mother who could always be counted on to cover for him, my father's slide into alcoholism and drugs was steady. At some stage in his life it was discovered that he was epileptic. Now he was on a diet of booze, drugs and a powerful anti-epileptic medication that created an extreme sensitivity to alcohol. This proved a potent cocktail and one which was to have a traumatic effect on all of our lives.

I was later to learn that Myra went to Durban, where she met Derek Merryweather. Very soon there was another child, a daughter called Jane. Jane was about three years old when Myra could no longer deny the emotional tug of Basil and Jenny. She left her new family and returned to Johannesburg, to Basil, Jenny and her mother-in-law. Basil persuaded Myra to try again: they were remarried and Myra soon fell pregnant with me.

But the old ways were deep rooted. It didn't take long to convince Myra that the Reynolds family had not changed. The boozing and consequent violence might even have escalated. In the circumstances, the last thing that Myra wanted was another baby to shackle her to the family. In a desperate attempt to subdue her unhappiness she drank exceptionally heavily throughout her pregnancy. There was no regard for the damage she might inflict on the innocent foetus that she carried so reluctantly. Her near-suicidal pact with alcohol continued until the day I was born and then afterwards to the day she died some twenty-five years later.

In April 1960, when she was in her eighth month, Myra got a telephone call from her mother, Evelyn. Once again Basil was out of work and the small family was staying at May's house in Great Britain Street.

"Myra, I've got to see you right away. It's important. Come now."

Myra could hear the urgency in her mother's voice. She put the phone down, took my sister's hand and started for the door.

"And just where do you think you're going?" May's voice was strident.

"That was my mother. She needs to see me."

"All right, but I'm coming with you." If there was any salacious gossip to be gleaned from the visit then May was determined to be the one who would pass it on. The two women, with Jenny in tow, hurried down Great Britain Street, round the corner and down the block or so to Evelyn Best's house.

The house was decrepit even by Kenilworth standards. Andrew and Evelyn Best had spent most of their income on alcohol and cigarettes. As a child Myra had frequently gone to school hungry and ill-shod, the butt of humiliating jokes and childish ridicule. Then Andrew Best committed suicide and Evelyn was left to manage as best she could. Over the years she had become emaciated and bedraggled, a lifetime of excess deeply etched on her yellowed skin and gaunt frame.

In the dingy bedroom they found Evelyn sitting on the edge of the bed still in her night-gown, one breast bare and pendulous in the half-light. She was strangely still as they walked in. Myra went to the bed and knelt in front of her mother. She took hold of her limp hand and felt beneath her fingers a tremulous jagged pulse beat. Jenny leaned against Myra's shoulder and watched as Evelyn took a bright coin out of her purse.

"This is all I have. I want Jenny to have it. Myra, I can't go on. Life is too hard."

She closed her eyes and fell over sideways onto the bed. Myra shrieked and clutched at her mother but Evelyn was dead, the bottle of ant poison still on the bedside table.

A month later, on 4 May 1960, I was born. This time May could not deny that I was Basil's child. The family resemblance was striking. Even she could see that I had both the cleft chin and the stocky build of my father. The situation must have been very unstable. It seems that there were constant quarrels about this second child and I have a feeling deep within my core that I was not wanted by either Myra or my father.

In the days after my birth Myra started a Baby Book for me. Reading through this slim book has given me the feeling that she was able to be a real mother to me for only a very short time. The first few pages of the book are lovingly and carefully filled in. At eighteen weeks I was hospitalised for the first time with a chest complaint. In the Baby Book Myra scrawled across the page "In Hospital". From then on there seems to have been a cessation of any motherly love she might have felt at the beginning. Perhaps, though, there is a clue to her feelings in the Baby Book. A small paragraph titled "Response to Music" indicates that even at that tender age I would respond to harmony. For my grandmother that was the ultimate delight, an indication that I would take after her. I wonder if, at this stage, May stepped in and claimed me for her own. Her firstborn, Douglas, was dead and his children beyond her grasp. Basil was lost to this silly girl and their firstborn too much like Myra for comfort. But the new baby, now there was an opportunity! From that moment I believe my destiny was defined: I lost my mother and became the possession of my grandmother, May Reynolds. And so, Myra lost not only her husband to his mother but both her children as well.

The climax came for Myra and Basil when, some months after I was born, Derek Merryweather came from Durban to Johannesburg to persuade Myra to go back to him and Jane.

Myra and Basil were then living in a flat in Rosettenville with Jenny and me. In a ferment of good intentions Basil had got himself a well-paid job and had moved his family into this small apartment well away from Great Britain Street. Myra was recovering from a bout of heavy drinking and was in bed when Derek arrived. And of course, May was there, her ubiquitous presence gorged with the potential for spontaneous emotional combustion.

"I've come to take Myra back to Durban with me. I need her and so does her daughter."

Basil was infuriated. "She's my wife and she stays here with me. No fucking stranger is going to walk into my house and make demands on my wife."

"That's right, Basil. You tell him what to do." May was, as usual, spoiling for a fight.

"Keep out of this, you stupid old woman, if you know what's good for you," Derek screamed at her.

"Basil, don't let him talk to your mother like that. Hit him, hit him." May was in her element, urging Basil on, creating another violent scene.

When my mother heard the raised voices she climbed out of bed and went through to the sitting room. Basil had begun to swing wild punches; one caught my mother on the breast and she fell. Jenny began screaming. She ran to the bassinet and picked me up. The adults were shrieking at each other and the two men had started to trade blows. Myra was on the ground with her head covered by her thin arms. She was crying. May sat back smiling with pleasure. She always liked a good fight, especially if someone else was throwing the punches. Jenny held me tight and slipped out of the apartment, determined to protect me from harm. Basil found her a few hours later sitting in a nearby park, her face streaked with tired tears and a sleeping baby clutched fiercely to her chest.

A few days later Myra left again. This time she took me with her. I was six months old. I am told that she went back to Durban, but whether she returned to Derek and Jane I don't know. Two weeks later there was a phone call at the Reynolds house. Jenny leaped up and ran to the phone. It was Myra.

"Jenny, darling, I just want you to know that I love you all very, very much."

May grabbed the phone out of Jenny's hand.

"Who the hell is that?" Myra put the phone down, and the next day Basil received a telegram, "Fetch Debbie".

The family went to Durban to retrieve me, May and Andy in the car with Jenny sitting in silence next to Basil who was so drunk that he knew neither where they were going nor why. They found me dirty, ragged and hungry and took me back to Great Britain Street. Myra was gone.

My sister Jenny has been able to fill in some of the gaps and I later learned that Myra met a young American seaman in Durban soon after she arrived there. Dell Hoffman was a chef on one of the United States Navy ships that called in at Durban in the sixties and seventies — and it's not difficult to imagine Dell falling for this young delicate woman with sad brown eyes. From the first Dell's devotion to Myra was complete: at last she had someone in her life to give her the peace and stability and love that she was longing for. Dell was only in Durban for a short while but at the end of his stay he persuaded her to leave behind her husband, her lover and her three little girls and go with him. Myra followed his ship to London and then to Hong Kong, where three years later she had Dell's son, Howard.

Somewhere along the way they went through a form of marriage. Whether Dell knew that Myra was still married to Basil Nicholls I don't know. Whatever the case, Myra and Dell lived together in Hong Kong for three or four years before he was transferred back to the United States. He took Myra and Howard to his home town of San Diego and a few years later Myra slipped across the border into Mexico to get a "quickie" divorce. She and Dell were married again, this time legally, and finally Myra had a modicum of stability and peace. There was no May Reynolds in her life — but, equally, there were no little girls to love. Myra was to spend the rest of her life grieving for the children she had abandoned. She also grieved for the weak, vacillating, handsome husband that she had left behind. There is no doubt in my mind that, although she had a great affection for Dell, Myra loved Basil until the day she died.

Dell was a wonderful person. Quiet, loving, solid. He gave Myra the love and the home that she needed and she was to live out the rest of her life in America. The next time I saw my mother was when I was thirteen years old.

As for my father — this story is as much about him as about me. He was weak, a pathetic drunk, often in jail because of his drinking, a child molester and a wife beater. And yet I loved him. I always believed that it was only when he had been drinking that he changed and became monstrous. But now, I don't know. I made the excuse that when sober he was totally unaware of what he had done, but now I can no longer be sure. I tried to convince myself that he was a good man turned rotten by his hatred for his mother, but that is no justification. Perhaps he was aware of what he was doing to me and to others. Perhaps he drank to try to obliterate from his mind what he really was. Perhaps he wasn't to blame for what he had become. And yet in spite of all he did to me I loved him and I believe, I hope, that there were times when he loved me as a father.

His mother loved him too. In May Reynolds' eyes Basil could do no wrong. Before my mother left it was always her "fault" that Basil drank. After she left it was her abandonment of him that "caused" my father's drinking. When Douglas was alive it was his fault that Basil drank, he was a bad "influence" on his younger brother. When Douglas died it was his murder that pushed Basil off the "straight and narrow". Basil grew up and grew old without ever learning to take responsibility for his own actions. May saw to it that he never had to. And instead of creating a loving bond between son and mother, this birthed a hatred that was so intense that Basil became an uncontrollable monster whom I feared with all of my small mind and body. Basil could not express his hatred for his mother in any other terms than those of violence against someone weaker or smaller than he was, his wife and his child and later other women.

Today I can pity him. At the time of these happenings my life was a see-saw of emotions — a deep love for him when he was sober and a hatred and fear for the beast that replaced him when he was drunk or drugged.

Poor Basil, always the "victim", always in some kind of trouble, never realising that he had the ability to make choices however hard that might have been, could have had a better life had he made the effort. He loved my mother and anguished all his life over her leaving. He blamed his mother and he blamed me that Myra had gone. The fault was his mother's and he "punished" her by his drunken behaviour. The fault was mine and he "punished" me by raping and prostituting me from the time I was six until I was fifteen.

Chapter 3

I lived with my grandparents, May and Andy Reynolds, my father Basil and my sister Jenny from the time they brought me back to Johannesburg when I was about six months old until I was thirteen.

I don't remember much about those early years, but I suppose I was much like any other child living in our street. I never really felt the loss of a mother when I was growing up. This was partly because no child in my environment, whether family members or neighbours, actually lived with parents. Except, of course, the Merediths across the road. They were different. On either side of the house in Great Britain Street were children living with grannies or aunts and uncles. My cousins, Stephen and Marion, were brought up by their grandmother, my aunt Caroline. Jenny and I were in the care of our grandparents. Even the two daughters of Tessa van Vuuren, Basil's common-law wife, were in the care of relatives.

I think, however, the main reason why I felt no maternal vacuum in my life was that my grandmother filled every facet of my existence. Granny May was the only constant in my troubled life. She brought me up, clothed and fed me, and made sure that I never forgot her magnanimity. My whole existence was dependent on her goodwill and she let me know, stridently and often, that I owed her "big time". In her possessiveness she even went so far as to legally adopt Jenny and me and change our names from Nicholls to Reynolds. My father had no say in the matter except to vent his speechless anger on me.

Kenilworth is south of Johannesburg and is generally regarded by many as being on the "wrong side of the tracks". But, in Andy's care, we had a life which was probably fairly normal for that part of the world. Basil was in and out of jobs, but so were many men in the neighbourhood. He was frequently up in front of a judge for some breach of the law, but then so were others in our area. His wife had run away with another man and had left him with two children, but there were others around us whose marital problems were similar or worse. Great Britain Street harboured many such sad stories.

My step-grandfather disliked me intensely, I knew that as instinctively as I knew when I was hungry or when the sun shone. I was an intrusion. I was the baby who cried at night, was sickly and dribbled over everything. Besides, he was already looking after one of Basil's children — and had done so uncomplainingly for many years. Andy adored Jenny, but then she was the first one he had sheltered. By the time I was foisted on him he was in his late fifties and I expect he had just had enough. Andy hovered on the periphery of our lives, largely silent, a husband and nominally head of the home, who was not allowed to participate in any of the family dramas. He was always there for the Nicholls family but he had a lot to endure.

At this time May's singing career was flourishing and she had engagements to sing almost every weekend at some night-club or party. She made quite a lot of money and this probably gave her an even greater sense of control over Andy and the rest of the family.

"May, why are you going out again tonight?" Andy would ask.

"I'm bringing home a lot of money, which is more than you can do, so shut up."

When May sang in the bars she would sometimes take Basil and me along to watch. It was on these occasions that I would see her happily instigate a barroom brawl and then expect Basil to finish it for her. He always reacted on cue and we would go home with Basil drunk and bleeding on the back seat of the car and May as darkly triumphant as Madame Defarge.

May showed a kindlier side to her nature when she went every second Saturday afternoon to Sterkfontein Psychiatric Hospital to sing to the patients. Some of the inmates were men who had come back from the war twenty years earlier with some sort of brain damage or with irreconcilable emotional problems. They would sit staring at me and my grandmother as she sang all the old wartime hits. "Wish me luck as you wave me goodbye" seemed particularly poignant under the circumstances. She also sang the latest songs and I remember one in particular, "Ma, he's making eyes at me", which they seemed to enjoy. Even today when I hear that song I can picture the rows of vacant-eyed men in green pyjamas who had been herded into the dining hall to listen to the "concert" and to shuffle their sad feet to the rhythm of the music.

After she had sung to the men May would parade through the different wards dragging me reluctantly behind her. I remember in particular the children's wards where I would surreptitiously stare at the hydrocephalic babies with their large heads and spider limbs all twisted and deformed and the cerebral palsied toddlers drooling and twitching in their cribs. I was probably too young to be exposed to such things, but May didn't seem to notice or care that I was distressed by what I witnessed. She was doing her "good deed" and that was all that mattered.

When I was about three there was one more furious argument between May and Andy.

"That child has to go, May. I'm tired of all this. I don't want the responsibility of another one of Basil's kids in the house anymore. So do something about it. Get rid of her. Force Basil to shoulder his responsibilities for once. Anything."

"Over my dead body will she go. If you don't like it, Andrew Reynolds, then you get the hell out."

Andy loved my grandmother too much to leave, so a compromise was reached and I was sent to a home run by nuns. I don't know where it was or how long I was there. All I remember was that I was so tiny that I couldn't get onto my bed without help. The nuns were kind to the little stray but some of the children were very cruel, as children can be. What I had to endure is mercifully blank but I remember coming out in a nervous itchy eczema so severe that the nuns asked May to remove me from the home.

One blustery day she and Andy arrived to take me back. The wind was lifting odd bits of paper and leaves from the front lawns as we walked away and I remember feeling swept along like another piece of detritus, of no more value than the papers and broken leaves swirling about in the dusty air. When she helped me into the back of the car May was complacent and Andy in a fit of silent fury. May had won and the unwanted child was being taken back to Great Britain Street. Andy wasn't able to express his disapproval of another mouth to feed except by ignoring me, which he did, wholeheartedly. I was not allowed on his lap, nor was I kissed and cuddled like Jenny. He adored Jenny, was proud of her, but only tolerated my presence. Once again I was the innocent pawn in a vortex of unspoken antagonisms.

Andy was very much under May's influence. He loved her, yes, but there was another reason beyond her arrogant domination that held him in bondage. Before Jenny was born May had fallen pregnant. Andy had been ecstatic. This was to be his first child, someone to carry on his name, his heritage, his blood, his gift to the world. Sometime in her third month, in a fit of drunken fury, Andy beat May so badly that she lost the child. He never forgave himself and it is probable that it was out of a sense of shame that he allowed May to do precisely what she wanted.

When Jenny was seventeen she met Jeffrey Booker and they fell in love and wanted to get married. Andy was devastated but there wasn't much he could do. Any warnings that Jenny was too young, too naive, were brushed aside as the maudlin meandering of an "outsider". May was enthusiastic and saw it as a personal victory, a vindication of all she had had to put up with. It also gave her an opportunity to show the neighbours just what a Reynolds could achieve when it came to pomp and ceremony. This was going to be her grand moment and in the excitement Jenny somehow got lost in the shadows of our grandmother's overbearing ego. A beautiful dress was bought, white with fairy-tale frills and satin roses. There was a crinoline petticoat of lace and hoops and, at three, I was small enough to fit under the skirt and cling to my sister's legs. When the time came for Jenny to leave for the church we found that she and her dress could not fit through the narrow garden gate. A few of the neighbourhood men obligingly lifted her over the wall and into the street.

The reception was held in our home and May and Stephen, my cousin, filled the house with boisterous music. Stephen was a professional musician and May adored him. Here was another family member to whom she could attach herself. Stephen was someone after her own heart, someone who knew and understood music, and he and Gran would often arrange jam sessions in our home. There were many evenings when the house would rumble and reverberate with musicians singing, playing, laughing, joking and drinking.

Those were good times but they were few. I was always excluded from the good times. As a small girl I would stand in the shadows, waiting to be called to make the tea or wash the dishes while the others were enjoying themselves. The only part I had of the "good" times was when it was at my expense. Otherwise I would stand on the side and watch them and wait.

But now Jenny was gone. Her marriage was a great loss to me. Now there was no longer anyone in the house to protect me from my grandmother, no one to help me change the bed sheets when I wet the bed, no one with whom I could feel safe and loved. I felt truly alone.

Even in those early days I lived in a constant fear of Granny May and the strap. She was known in the neighbourhood as a spiteful harridan, respectable according to the norms of Great Britain Street, but still a woman that no one would cross. Many times the neighbours conspired to protect me from her wrath. If I spent a few hours playing at the home of some child in the street and Granny May wanted me home to wash the dishes or make her tea, she would stand at the gate and whistle for me like a dog. Everyone knew that whistle and what it meant. Word would pass along the street that May was looking for Debbie to come home and I would be warned to scarper back as quickly as possible. More than once when I was tardy she fetched the strap to me and beat me all along the street. I remember a particular time when an irate neighbour rushed out and barred the way.

"May, that's no way to treat a child. You've no cause to beat her like that."

"How dare you tell me what I can or cannot do. This child is mine and I'll do what I like with her. Don't interfere with me, d'you hear? And here's something for you to think about." With that May turned her furious lashing onto the neighbour and began to beat her instead. I escaped into the house and watched from a safe distance, too humiliated to stay in public view.

May's confrontations with the neighbours always ended in violence. She would lash out at other women with her fists or tweak their noses or in some other physical way get the better of them. Then she would chortle with delight at having humiliated them. People in the street learned very quickly to stay out of the Reynolds' affairs.

Growing up in that environment of violence and with my repressed emotions of hate, anger, frustration and guilt I was the perfect patsy. May constantly reminded me that I was only in her house on sufferance and I grew up feeling unwanted and responsible for all the bad things that went on in the home. I grew up believing that I deserved to be punished for being alive, for being in my grandmother's house, for eating her food, for having to be clothed. May told me often and shrilly that I was bringing her to poverty and ruin, so when the punishment came it seemed only what I had earned.

Chapter 4

The first time it happened was in the early spring of 1966. The few trees in Great Britain Street were full of pale green buds that promised to turn, in a week or so, into large fluted leaves that we children could sail down the gutters when they flooded with summer rain. In the small garden in front of the house a bedraggled jasmine spread its meagre growth over the wall and three or four rose bushes elbowed one another up the side of the house. These rose bushes were the pride of my grandmother and I was not allowed near them in case I should take some liberty such as stopping to inhale their delicate perfume or touching their calm and silky buds.

Just before the spring rains May and Andy left for a short holiday on the south coast of Natal. It was the first time that they had been away without one or other of the family tagging along with them. Usually they would have been burdened with either Jenny or myself and very often my father and Tessa as well. This time May insisted that she and Andy needed a break from the rigours of their exhausting family and left me in the care of my father and the ever-silent Tessa.

I missed Jenny. Before her marriage she had been the one person in Great Britain Street of whose love I was certain. She was fourteen when I was born, so there had been little companionship between us during our childhood, but instead there was always the protection of a big sister when life got too volatile for me. Jenny was always safe in the loving protection of Andy — although no one escaped May's domination and she was as fearful of Gran as I was. My father must have been aware that Jenny was out of bounds. He would never have touched her, knowing that Andy would have had no compunction in breaking his neck if he did so. I was less fortunate. Andy made it obvious that he did not care for me, that I was a burden he could well do without. His inability to love and protect me at that time made me desperately vulnerable to Basil's predatory nature.

And, of course, there was Fanny. Fanny was a tall, rangy, very black woman who acted as our domestic servant and often as my ally and protector. Fanny seemed to have caught the Reynolds malady, a predilection for alcohol in large and destructive quantities. She was more often drunk than sober and, perhaps because of that, may not have felt the lashing bite of May's leather belt when she stood between me and my raging grandmother.

"Now, you come and eat before the Missus comes in and catches you again." Fanny felt the need to fatten me up and often she would scavenge a small titbit from the kitchen after one or the other of us had experienced a particularly savage beating. I loved Fanny.

I also loved Tessa. Tessa's husband had been Basil's best friend and drinking partner in the early years just after the war. After his death she somehow drifted into Basil's life and lived with him, knowing who and what he was and yet remaining loyal to him to the end of her days. Tessa obviously adored my handsome father with a deep-rooted intensity in spite of his alcoholism, his violent temper, his frequent prison spells and his passionate and consuming hatred of his mother. She bore the silent scars of many brutal beatings from Basil. Those beatings were often meant for me or Jenny but Tessa would rush in and stand between us and a father who knew no boundaries. She was a silent waif of a woman, dark haired, with the scars of many savage attacks and much inner pain on her face.

The house in Great Britain Street was no tender refuge. Behind stolid face-brick walls and dingy curtains our private tragedy played itself out. There was a secrecy about the doings of the Reynolds family. Granny May had a sense of pride when it came to "prying" neighbours and none knew what tempests blew behind our walls, although they may have guessed. It didn't seem to matter what went on behind those greying net curtains as long as nobody in the neighbourhood knew about it.

In the early part of 1966 Basil had been out of work for months. In normal and happier times, which seemed few and far between, he worked as a welder and was, May boasted, very good at his job. But when he went to work drunk or when his uncontrollable temper created vicious scenes at the workplace, he would be told none too gently to leave ... or else. This particular spring Basil had found work with a building contractor and now there were coins jingling a catchy tune in his pocket, begging to be spent at the local bar.

It was a Friday afternoon and Basil had knocked off work early. He had probably spent several hours in one sleazy barroom after another, visiting the "friends" whom he had not seen in his dry and workless months and buying round after round with noisy abandon. In the late afternoon he staggered back to May's house, snot running out of his nose and vomit staining his shirt and pants. He collapsed on the nearest bed and fell into a noisy sleep. Fanny was nowhere to be seen. Tess and I were alone and we both ardently hoped that Basil would sleep well, for it was the only time we could be sure of safety.

At some stage Tessa had decided that the only way to stop my father's self-destruction was to take his money away. At the time it seemed like a good idea but she was too afraid to do it. Her jaw had been broken not once but twice and consequently her face had a slightly lopsided appearance. One eye drooped faintly and there was a puckered scar above the other, both relics of attacks from my father. Already I had learned that the natural follow-up to one of Basil's alcoholic benders was that there would be fighting and screaming, things would be thrown and finally someone would be hurt, badly hurt. That person was usually Tessa. There would be blood and crying and it always terrified me. I would have done anything to avoid that. If it meant my creeping up to him while he snored through his drunken sleep, rifling his pockets and stealing his money, then I would do that too.

"Debbie, you creep into the room and take the money out of his pocket and then we'll go to the shop and get something for supper. I'll even get you a sweet." Tessa gave me a gentle shove. I put my worn teddy bear on the floor and crept as quietly as I could into the room. The window was closed and the air smelled stale. A late afternoon sun painted slices of pale light over the floor and onto the bed where Basil lay snoring loudly, his mouth open and his jacket half under his slack body. I crept closer. This was going to be difficult. His wallet jutted out of the pocket that he lay on. Slowly, slowly I slid my hands into the pocket and started to pull.

Basil grunted sloppily and turned in his sleep, trapping my small hands under his body. He felt me there and woke up.

"You little shit. What th' hell d'you think you're doing?" He pulled my hands out of the jacket and then he knew. "Stealing my money, are you? I'll show you what you get for that!" He rolled off the bed and, using his steel-capped welding boots, began to kick me in the stomach and then in the back as I turned to run out of the room.

"Tess, Tess!" he screamed after me. "Where's that stupid bitch. Tess! I'll show you lot who's boss around here. Tess!" Basil came screaming and lurching down the passage after me.

"Basil, leave Debbie alone. It's not her fault. Leave her alone." Tessa ran to stand between me and my father's boots. Basil grabbed at her head and came away with a clump of hair. He swung his great fists at her, pummelling her face with both hands. As I slipped away I saw her nose erupt, the blood splashing down her dress and smearing across Basil's fists.

Then suddenly Fanny was there. In the blur of the moment she, or someone, grabbed my arm and ran with me down the passage, through the kitchen, with Basil roaring behind us. Hands pushed me under the car. A voice whispered, "Stay there, Debbie, else he'll kill you." I saw running feet, back to the house.

I crawled out from the oily dirty space. Someone had to rescue Tessa. Basil was going to kill her this time and it was my fault. The kitchen floor had smears of blood all over and Tessa was lying there, her eyes closed and blood pouring from her ears, nose and mouth. She was dead, she had to be dead with all that blood everywhere.

"Bitchbitchfuckingcuntbitch." His fists in her face, his welding boots everywhere, back, stomach, breasts, kidneys. No expression on his dark face. Controlled. Words coming close together. Fists and feet tattooing on her body.

"Leave her, Daddy. Leave her. Stop. Stop!"

Finally he moved away from her and staggered out of the kitchen and into the back yard. I peered through the window and saw that he was sitting on the front seat of his car drinking something from a bottle. I bent over Tessa, my arms went around her.

"Tess, please don't be dead. Please, don't be dead."

She moved, rolled over and got to her knees.

"Tess, come to my room, I'll hide you. I won't let Daddy hit you again. I promise. Tess, I'm sorry. It's all my fault. It's all my fault."

Tess managed, somehow, to get to my bedroom and I shut the door, hoping that she would be safe. Fanny was in her room in the back yard. She was obviously not so drunk that she didn't know she was safer behind a locked door. I was alone with my father and he was looking for someone to beat, someone to blame.

He came back into the house and started banging on the doors and screaming for Tessa. This time he would kill her, I was sure. This time it would be over for her. I walked down the passage towards my father holding onto the wall for support. He grabbed hold of my hair, yanked me off my feet and dragged me down the passage and into the lounge.

"It's all your fault, you little ...! It's you that's caused all this unhappiness. Why? Why have you done this?"

"Daddy, I'm sorry. I'm sorry, Daddy."

"No, you're not. You're just like your bitch mother. You're out to hurt me just like your fucking mother."

"I'm not, Daddy. Please, I'm not."

"And your grandmother. You bloody women. You're all alike. Out to get me, the lot of you."

By this time Basil was beyond rage. His face was grey with a thin line of white around his mouth, saliva running down his chin from the side of those pale rigid lips. I was to learn this sign, over the next seven years. He was no longer drunk in a way that I could, even then, identify. There was no falling over, no slobbering, no slurred words. No expression in his eyes.

"I hate your mother. I hate that woman. She's against me. Everyone's against me. Nobody understands how I feel. All you women are the same. Got the knee in for me. All the time. All the time. Christ, I hate you all."

He grabbed me by my shoulders, each finger creating a blister of pain. I was crying but he didn't seem to notice. I was too scared to call out, to tell him to stop. If I did then Tess would come out and it would start all over again. All I could think of was — please, Daddy, don't hurt Tessa again.

"I was never good enough for your mother, that's why she left me. And I'm not good enough for your grandmother either. Why can't she just leave me alone? Dammit, why can't she just leave me the hell alone? And it's all your fault. If it wasn't for you I'd be out of here."

"Daddy, I'm sorry. Daddy, I'm sorry."

"No, you're not. And I'll show you what you get for being a bad girl. I'll show you."

He pushed me down on the carpet, its large red and gold pattern pressed into my cheek. He pulled off my dress and then my panties. Then he opened my legs and raped me.

It was horror and pain and panic. The pain was excruciating. I was small, with a straight up and down body. He was tearing me in half. I was too small for this thing he was pushing into me. This wasn't my daddy, this was a monster from my worst and darkest nightmare. His eyes were staring down at me and I saw myself in their yellow sunflower burst. This wasn't my daddy, this was a wild animal staring down at me, panting and slobbering. Killing me. This wasn't me, this was some bad, bad person who needed to be punished. It can't be me. Move out, Debbie, move out and go where you'll be safe until it's all over. I wanted to scream, to beg him to stop. My mouth made the words but the words wouldn't come. "No, Daddy, no, Daddy. Stop. Please. You're hurting me." If I screamed, if I made a noise, then Tess would come in and get this. Keep quiet and take Tessa's punishment. You deserve to. You're bad, Debbie, you're bad.

He pulled away from me. I thought it was over but he thrust his penis into my mouth.

"Suck it, you filthy bitch. Suck it or this time I'll really hurt you."

I didn't know what he wanted me to do. I put my lips around that thing and sucked at it. This wasn't my Daddy. This had to be someone else. Not my Daddy who said he loved me. I wasn't Debbie. This wasn't happening. I was someone else, somewhere else. This couldn't be happening. It was too sore to be happening.

He began to lick me all over. His saliva was full of the smell of alcohol and vomit and that sweet stuff he smoked. All over my body. My neck, my non-existent breasts, my stomach. I became sticky with spit and gin and dagga. He licked me between my legs and tried to stick that thing into me again. Finally he got off me and went to his room, fell onto the bed and went back to sleep.

I lay curled up in a small bundle. Who was there that I could cry for? Not my mother. She was long gone. My mother had left because of me, they all told me that, because I was such a stupid child, always sick, always needy, always bad, and so the words couldn't come, "Mommy, Mommy." I couldn't cry for my grandmother either. She had enough troubles, she had to look after me and I was just in the way, stopping her from enjoying all the good things she wanted.

I whimpered softly, "Teddy bear, Teddy bear."

Slowly I got up and walked with wide-apart legs to the bathroom. There was blood everywhere. I couldn't use the face cloth; somebody would see the blood and want to know what had happened. If anybody knew what I'd just done, the bad thing I'd done, then they would get angry with me, blame me and beat me. I pulled off a lot of toilet paper from the toilet roll behind the door and tried to wipe the blood away.

Tessa was barely conscious when I eventually went back to my room. Blood had run down from her ears and mouth and stuck to her hair. Her eyes were almost closed and her nose puffy and skew. I wondered if she knew what had happened to me, because she pushed herself up and staggered to the phone. She dialled my Aunt Caroline's number and asked her to send someone to fetch me.

"No, Tess. I can't leave you. Daddy will hurt you again. I must be here to save you."

"Go, Debbie, or else he'll kill you. Go while you can."

Tessa took my hand, whether to comfort me or for support I don't know. Together we tiptoed down the passage. As I passed my teddy bear I bent down and scooped it up, cradling it closely, walking with pain almost too much to bear. If we went out of the back door its screeching hinges would wake Basil. So we went into the lounge where a few minutes ago I had been lying. Tessa lifted me up and pushed me through the burglar bars in the fanlight of the side window. Caroline's husband, Uncle Tom, was there and I fell into his waiting arms. A moment later Tessa pushed teddy through the window and I caught him as he fell.

I had been raped by my father and I was six years old.

Chapter 5

And so my father, Basil Nicholls, became a monstrous feature in my small life. He would come and go like some tormented shade, forever about his dubious business; sometimes in prison, sometimes sleeping at home and often sleeping with the tramps and hoboes in central Johannesburg. He was such a paradox, there were times when he would arrive at May's house impeccably dressed, shoes polished to a mirror shine, tie exactly and fashionably knotted. The next time he would confound us all by returning dirty, decrepit, smelling of the garbage in which he had been lying. The only time we could be reasonably sure of seeing him was when he had been in a brawl or had been arrested for possession of drugs or for drunken driving. At these times my grandmother would patch him up or bustle down to the police station to "make things right" for her boy. Then she would make sure I knew what a rotten father he was.

"That's your father all over," she would say with morose satisfaction. "Been at the booze again and look where it gets him. Damned bloody rotten, that's what he is."

It was at these times that I was in mortal danger. After the first rape I learned very quickly that when Basil had been drinking May would invariably begin to criticise and nag him. There would be a fight and then he would reach for me in the dark and shadowed night. He knew he was safe from discovery. May and Andy would take a sleeping pill before they went to bed, and after that the nights were his. My body would become a bloody battleground as he vented his fury and frustration on my defenceless frame. Many times in his drunken rage he would penetrate me with anything at hand, beer bottles, hairbrush handles, anything. My only defence was to withdraw the core psyche of myself from the awful moment and wait, blind and passive, for his fury to pass. Then I would crawl away, wash myself as best I could and creep into my own bed and try to get some sleep.

I started school the year.after his attacks began and often I would arrive in the mornings too sore from my father's depraved attention to sit on the wooden school chair. I would squirm and shift trying to find a way to sit that would not press too painfully on my invaded parts.

"Debbie," the teacher would say in plain exasperation, "can't you sit still for even five minutes?"

At school I became known as a troubled child who suffered inexplicable bouts of quiet withdrawal alternating with wild, uncontrollable aggression. I bit my nails until my fingers were bloody. My school work was bad and I found difficulty in concentrating and remembering what I had been taught.*

My thoughts were too full of my home experiences for anything else to matter very much. Also, I knew I couldn't do schoolwork; everybody at home always said I was dumb, and here was the proof — and there was little incentive from my family to work hard, to try. It was not in my grandmother's nature to praise or reward and I was therefore unaware at the time that somewhere deep inside there was a hungry intelligence waiting to be fed by a sensitive and sympathetic teacher. I was not to find such a person until I was twelve years old and I met Ruth Nielsen.

At this time there was a family living across Great Britain Street who became my refuge and sanctuary. Jill and Tommy Meredith had three children, Carol, John and Richard. Their lives were very different from anything I knew. There was a mummy and a daddy and a bunch of kids. For me that was unusual and I was intrigued. Soon I was invited to go over and play — slowly I was drawn into their lives and made to feel one of them. Aunt Jill's house became my retreat from the storms of violence and sexual attack in my own home. I spent weekends with them and still remember the mornings when the kids would creep down the passage and burst into Jill and Tommy's bedroom. Then all four children, plus a cat or two, would bundle in together in the sleepy warmth of their bed for a morning cuddle. I had special clothes that Aunt Jill had bought me that I wore only when I was at their house. And presents at Christmas time! Christmas was magical. We put milk and biscuits out for Father Christmas and breathlessly promised that we wouldn't sleep a wink all night. The Merediths were the only people who ever gave me presents without any conditions attached and I loved them as unconditionally as they loved me.

One Saturday morning the Meredith kids and I climbed onto their roof to try out a mischievous new game. We sat on a piece of cardboard and slid down the steep side of the roof — the trick was not to fall off when we hit the guttering. If we did the fall was not high or particularly dangerous, and

*These are some of the symptoms of an abused child. A list of other symptoms can be found in *When your child has been molested* by Kathryn Hagens and Joyce Case.

it was great fun until one of the neighbours ran to call May.

"Oh my God, May. Debbie's up on the Merediths' roof."

Gran dashed across the road armed with the leather belt that hung behind the kitchen door. My leather belt, the one she used to tame me.

"Debbie, come down this instant." She must have thought I was fool enough to get down from the comparative safety of the roof, and I knew there was no way she could get up there to pull me off. I was safe, for the moment, at least. When she got tired of waiting for me she yelled, "You've got to get down sometime, and when you do I'll be waiting with the strap."

Slowly I crept down, but before she could carry out her threat there was a phone call to say that Basil had been taken to the J G Strijdom Hospital. He had been in a fight and suffered a terrible beating. May was in a ferment of concern and the roof episode was forgotten for the time being. Sooner or later, I knew, she would remember and give me the lambasting she had promised me.

Basil was lying in the casualty ward with easily the largest, most vicious shiner we had ever seen. It hung like a ball from his face, purple and throbbing. He was still quite drunk and very aggressive. He had hit one of the nurses with his fists and was making life so difficult for the staff that, by the time Granny May and I arrived, they were ready to throw him out on the street. We took him home but on the way he had to stop at the bottle store where, in spite of Granny's protestations, he bought several bottles of brandy.

"Daddy, what happened to you?"

"Don't bother your father now, Debbie. Can't you see he doesn't want to deal with you right now?"

"But, Daddy, what happened to you?"

"Yes, Basil, while you were fighting all over town I had to deal with this daughter of yours. Do you know what she's up to when your back is turned? On the Merediths' roof, playing Superman, if you don't mind. Really, Basil, I can't manage any more. It's time you stepped in here and acted like a father."

"Daddy, what happened?"

He turned to me. "I was on a roof and I fell off."

I believed him, and somehow felt that I was to blame for this and all the other horrible things that happened in Basil's life. I knew with the instinct of an unhappy child that all the bad things that happened in everybody's life around me were because of me, because I existed.*

That night Basil insisted that I sleep with him and I got the punishment I "deserved" for being on the Merediths' roof. My punishment was another night of rape.

I believe that the Merediths knew nothing about the sexual abuse, violence and the drink that haunted my life, although I'm sure they suspected that all was not well with me. I must have been a fairly appealing little creature at that time because Jill and Tommy decided that they would like to adopt me. When I was about eight years old they went to the Social Welfare people and presented their case. Granny May always told anyone who would listen how poverty stricken she was, really battling, and how difficult it was with this child. Now the Merediths told the Welfare people, "May Reynolds can't manage. We have a place for the child in our home and in our hearts and we would like to do the right thing."

Papers were drawn up and the children were ecstatic. Another sister! How wonderful! Then the Merediths went to May.

"Over my dead body will you take this child away from me!" she shouted.

"But," protested Tommy, "You know that you can't give her what she needs. You're always telling us how poor you are and how you can't afford to look after another grandchild."

"Like hell will you busybodies take her away. She's mine and she stays here where she belongs."

Sadly Tommy and Jill turned away, tore up the papers, and left me under the authority of my grandmother. Shortly after that they bought a farm on the outskirts of Krugersdorp and moved away from Great Britain Street. The house on the farm was warm and friendly, with chintz curtains and flowers in vases. There were chickens and horses, eggs to be collected and cows to be milked, a real farm. I was often a guest there but there was never the same camaraderie as there had been in Great Britain Street. Granny May had seen to that by her rudeness to the Merediths and her determination to maintain control over me.

We moved to Natal when I was nine years old and I lost contact with these wonderful people. My only link with a normal and sane family was lost and I felt betrayed. In my young mind it seemed as if they had stopped loving

---

*Whenever there is a major deficit in parental love, the child will, in all likelihood, respond to that deficit by assuming itself to be the cause of the deficit, thereby developing an unrealistically negative self-image.
People of the lie, by M Scott Peck, p. 60.

me. I couldn't understand why; they were the only real family that I had. I was confused at my loss, not knowing then how to maintain contact with them. I had trusted them, loved them and believed in their power to make things right in my life, but they were gone. I promised myself then that I would never trust or love anyone again.

School was a torment. There was no one in my peer group to whom I felt close. Perhaps my experiences, even then, separated me from other little girls. Also I was the most financially impoverished one in the class. May had seen to it that everybody in the school knew what a martyr she was to have taken on this child. She was, of course, ever present and exceedingly popular with the principal and staff.

Granny May could always be relied on to raise funds for any new project at the school. Whenever something was needed, curtains for the hall, books for the library, she would "put on a show". I wanted this to stop. I hated her ubiquitous presence in my life. Even my school life was not free of her.

I would have done anything to make my grandmother disappear. One morning I went to school looking suitably crestfallen. "Debbie," my teacher bent down to look at me, "whatever's the matter?"

"Miss, it's my grandmother. She died last night." I hoped that my face was sufficiently tragic.

"Oh my heavens. How terrible. How terrible. Poor May Reynolds." The teacher made an excuse to leave the classroom and ran with the dreadful news to the principal and secretaries.

"Oh heavens! What an angel she was. We'll miss her so much."

"We must start a fund for the funeral, get some flowers. Oh dear, whatever will that poor little girl do."

My grandmother chose that moment to phone the school and I was branded a liar and a troublemaker merely for pretending what I wanted so desperately — her total obliteration.

Granny May went once a week to a hairdresser in Regents Park. Typically, she became bosom-buddies with many of the women clientele and many happy hours were spent gossiping about whoever wasn't in the "salon" at the time. She got particularly friendly with the hairdresser, who was Henri in the shop and Harry Ludick in the little house adjacent, which he shared with his ailing mother. It wasn't long before May discovered that Henri was into seances.

May was excited. At last she had found a way to contact her mother, Warren and Douglas, especially Douglas. Even in death it seemed that she couldn't let go of her son Douglas. Each week after having her hair mar-celled into tight little waves at the salon she would take me by the hand and walk with Henri to the house to meet over the seance table with Mrs Ludick and the "spirits".

May had been interested in the occult long before I was born and now she carried her obsession with the spirit world from the hairdressing salon into our house. There were times when Basil and Tessa were staying with us and I would have to share May's bed while Andy gently snored in his bed across the room. I remember occasions when she would start up out of a deep sleep.

"Debbie, don't move. My mother's here." Peering over the edge of the blankets, I dreaded what I might see, my eyes feeling the size of breakfast cups and my heart beating a frightened rhythm. Of course there was noth-ing.

"My legs! I can't move my legs. They're sitting on my legs. Debbie, go and fetch the Bible."

According to Granny May, Douglas and other members of her family were constantly in and out of the house, sometimes sitting on the bottom of our bed, apparently with nothing better to do with their afterlife than visit an old lady and her terrified grandchild.

One weekend we went with Harry and his mother to Carletonville to visit his family. This was the town where some years previously several of the houses had disappeared into a sinkhole and one family had died. Harry's family took us to the site of the tragedy and we stood around with Granny May in a frenzy of delight at being at the place where this terrible thing had taken place. A seance was suggested but saner heads prevailed and we left with May darting eager glances backwards, hoping perhaps that a spirit would ascend from the pit. Granny May was one of those people drawn by tragedy like a moth to a flaming candle. She would stand around a car acci-dent with a smile on her face discussing in minute detail the injuries or deaths. She always had to be where the suffering was.

I wonder what she would have said had she been aware of the tragedy play-ing itself out in her own home.

Chapter 6

In 1969, the year I turned nine, something happened that was to change
our lives completely — Andy had a stroke. He and I were alone in the
house one evening when Granny May and Stephen had gone to a movie.
There was such a distance between us that we sat through the evening in
silence, each in our private world. We went to bed fairly early and I was
wakened by a loud crash. I turned on the light and saw that Andy had fall-
en out of bed.

He couldn't speak, couldn't tell me what was wrong. Instead he indicated
to me that he needed to urinate. I ran for the chamber pot and helped him
relieve himself. His humiliation was palpable but for me it was nothing to
handle him. I was used to touching a man and knew what to do. I had
already had three years of my father. Andy had wet himself so I found him
clean pyjamas and put a pillow under his head and a blanket over his legs.
I held his hand while he dozed restlessly and together we waited for
Granny May to come home.

A great joy and feeling of confidence surged through me. I had been the
one to help Grandpa. I wasn't a useless brat. At last I had done something
that couldn't be criticised. I was a help when it was most needed. I had
made it all right for him.

Andy's stroke changed everything. Doctors told May that he needed to be
at the seaside, so the house in Great Britain Street was sold and we moved
to Munster on the south coast of Natal. May rented a cottage that was part
of a holiday complex fairly close to the beach. We were the only family living there on a semi-permanent basis, so the place had a bleak, hollow feel
to it. I hated the rows of empty windows, and the long walk through wild-
ly growing hedges of poinsettias to the bus stop every morning. I hated the
school in Margate. I hated not having anybody to play with in the afternoons. I hated being so far away from Jenny. In fact, I hated everything
about Munster. Being close to the beach made little difference to me as I

wasn't allowed to play there unless an adult was with me and Granny May was too busy with Andy to bother.

With this move May's singing career virtually came to an end. Audiences on the south coast were sparse except during the school holidays when the "Vaalies" would flood down to the seaside. All she had left was a sickly husband and the burden of a nine year old grandchild. Basil and Tessa were still in Johannesburg, so for the moment I was safe from my father's attentions.

The house was smaller than the one we had left in Great Britain Street. There was one damp bedroom in which May and Andy slept. In the lounge there was a small truckle bed for me that folded away during the day. Granny May had her precious red lounge suite with the hideous ball and claw legs that were so much like her own. At night I skulked invisibly behind the sofa in my fold-down bed. There was no dining room and we had to eat in the kitchen crowded between the stove and the refrigerator. There was, however, a sunny porch where Andy could be left dozing in an old chair while I went to school. Granny May employed a Zulu man who came in every day to help with Andy but when Josiah wasn't around she got very impatient with Andy's slow fumbling and would often take the belt to him. The only time I ever stood up to her was when she beat Andy in my presence. I flung myself in front of him screaming, "Don't you hit my Grandpa." The belt cut through the air and the next day I went to school with a split lip and bleeding welts on both arms.

Very early one morning, long before the pewter hours of dawn, I woke up with a rancid taste in my mouth. A hard grey pain somewhere in my middle had begun to spread tendrils through my body and my face felt clammy with heat. Beyond the lounge I could hear the faint surging of the sea and a sharp night wind had crept through the window and was tugging nervously at the curtains. In their bedroom Andy and May slept heavily, each with their own noisy rhythm. I crept out of bed, padded along the passage to the bathroom and sat on the floor. It wasn't a good idea to turn on the bathroom light because that would wake Granny May and then I would get a belting for being out of bed.

I knelt down between the bath and the toilet and felt the cold wall tiles through the thin material of my pyjamas. If I pressed my head against them I could draw in their coolness and that felt good. Kind of soothing after the hot bed. I wished that I could just sit like that, in the comforting dark, and not have to get up again. Then the pain clutched more fiercely and I vomited noisily into the toilet. The light switch clicked, flooding the small bathroom with cold white light. From the floor Granny May looked monstrous, legs like old trees, blue-veined with gnarled toes rooted into the floor. Her stiff body towered over me and through my pain and fear I saw her arms lengthen like spiders as they reached across the bathroom and grabbed my shoulder. I should have felt her hard fingers pressing into me but there seemed a growing distance between my body and my mind, the normal sharpness now woolly and indistinct. I heard her voice as if from a far-off place.

"What the hell are you doing out of bed? Haven't I told you not to go wandering around after I've put you to bed? Really, Debbie, this is all too much. What with Andy and you to look after, I'm a nervous wreck." She grabbed hold of me, hauling me upright, and pushed me down the passage and into her bed. Andy, in his bed in the corner of the room, slept on, his wet snores an even metronome in the dark.

"And where the hell's your father? Doesn't he ever take responsibility for you? No, leaves it all to me, he does. He's never around. How'm I supposed to handle all this?"

I edged onto the side of the bed. Silence was my only defence but, as always, it was probably interpreted as dumb insolence. The pain in my stomach had dimmed after I had retched in the bathroom but now it returned and pulsated along my legs and into my chest. The pain had largely dissipated by morning but just before dawn I had been sick once more, managing to stumble to the bathroom in time, fear of what Granny May would do adding stealth as I crept down the cool passage.

The morning was bright and, even at breakfast time, a heat haze trembled over the unkempt back garden. Since his stroke Andy had to be fed and I was given the task of ladling porridge, toast and coffee into his skewed mouth and wiping the excess that dribbled over his chin. It was a task that gave me a sense of importance, for it seemed that at last I was able to do something right. Every morning I would also put on Andy's socks and shoes and brush his thinning hair before I left for school.

Through my careful attention a special attachment had formed between my step-grandfather and me. I knew that Andy had never loved me but now the old man had become dependent on me and I was there to make things right for him. His mind was not as sharp as it had once been and he couldn't speak very well. His mouth sagged and his movements were shuffling and uncertain. But now it was almost as if we bonded because of our mutual helplessness. Over the weeks and months he grew to love me and I him. Sometimes we would go for a walk in the garden together, Andy tottering on shaky legs and me in solicitous attendance. In the evenings we would kneel down together at the side of his bed and say our prayers: "God bless GrandpaandGrannyandJennyandTessa — andDaddy — andme."

This particular morning in February as I fed Andy a grey lassitude crept into my joints and I found difficulty in lifting my hands.

"May, the child. Sick," I heard Andy say.

"Jesus, I've got so much to do. What the hell did I do to deserve all this? Haven't I enough to bear without Debbie getting sick as well?" May put a large hand on my forehead. "Hm, well I suppose you're right for once. I'd better get her to the doctor. Now I have to spend time sitting at the doctor's. Don't I have enough with Andy sick all the time? Where'm I to find the money if you're sick too? And where's Basil when I need him? Nowhere to be found, of course. Nowhere. I have to shoulder all his responsibilities."

The next few hours were a blur. I remember the rough car ride from Munster to the Port Shepstone hospital, the gentle hands of the nurses in the ward as they prepared me for surgery and then, much later, waking up in a large hospital bed with my side blazing with pain. For two or three days I drifted in and out of sleep, only sometimes aware that my grandmother was there and once being almost sure that Basil was holding my hand. Tessa also appeared in the periphery of my vision and stood, as usual, a silent shadow behind Granny May's large and domineering presence.

The nurses were full of compassion for May. Here she was, battling to keep this family together, with no money and no support other than a small pension. And still she came all the way, 72 kilometres there and back, to visit this child. What a charitable angel, what a saint. Were they talking about the same Granny that I knew so well? The nursing staff loved Granny May for her "selfless" devotion to her family and in turn Granny May loved their cooing sympathy. Outward appearances were everything to May and she strove hard to maintain a facade of respectability, no matter what devilish deeds were whirling about underneath.

Basil held my hand and I watched him through half-drugged eyes, wondering at the bandage over his head. Strange, he must have come back while I was in hospital.

"She's your responsibility, Basil. She's your child, not mine." When it was convenient Granny May forgot that she had insisted on legally adopting me. "It's time you started behaving responsibly towards her. You can't expect me to go on, you know. I won't be around for ever."

"Yes, Mom." Basil's voice was strained.

"You're a fine one. Where were you when she got sick and had to have her appendix out? Where were you when we had to rush her to hospital? I've got Andy to look after. I can't be everywhere, you know."

"Hell, Mom, I've only been out a week. Have a heart, man."

"Well, one of these days they won't open the doors and let you out and then where will I be? Left looking after your child, I suppose. It's not good enough, Bas. You ought to love your child more. You ought to show her you love her."

"I do, Mom. I do."

"I don't need this in my life, Bas. It's bad enough with Andy sick. And now the child's going to have to have someone to fetch and carry for her. How often do you come to me cap in hand when you're in trouble? But when I need you, no sir, you're nowhere around."

"OK, Mom. OK. Enough. I'm trying, Mom."

A few days later Granny May brought Andy to see me. I was well enough to be sitting up in bed and smiling when he shuffled towards me. He had a small box in his hand.

"Here," he said. "For you."

I was puzzled. Andy had never given me anything before. I tore at the wrappings. It was a small gold and black watch with a jolly round face. I clutched it in both hands and looked at Andy in amazement. "For me?"

He nodded, a lopsided grin on his face. I put my arms out and he bent down for a brief hug. "Thank you, Grandpa. I promise I'll look after it. I'll wear it till the day I die."

"No more sick," he said.

"No, no more. I promise."

A few days later Granny May came to fetch me.

"Where's my father? Why didn't he come to fetch me?"

"Where do you think he is? Where he always is — in the pub. Again. I suppose I'm going to have to look after him like I always have to. I seem to be the only one in this family who can do anything right. Really, I don't know any more."

I remember pressing myself back into the seat of the car, wishing that I could make myself so small that nobody would find me, ever again. Only the feel of the new watch on my wrist was real. That and the subdued pain in my side. The doctor in the hospital said I'd been brave, but I didn't feel brave. I just felt tired and sad, because once again I had displeased Granny May without knowing what I had done wrong.

Basil was at the house in Munster when we got back from the hospital. He came to the car and took my arm. "Well, look who's back. Daddy's little girl. All in one piece." He laughed unsteadily. "Well, almost in one piece."

"Basil, stop making a fool of yourself and take the child's things." Granny

May hauled my small suitcase out of the car and thrust it at Basil. He bent down to kiss me and I could smell the alcohol on his breath and also the sweet smell of that stuff he smoked. I knew what that meant and wished with all my nine year old heart that there was somewhere I could be where I would be safe from what was coming.

I knew the signs. They were always the same. When my father had been drinking and smoking that stuff and when he took his pills on top of all the rest then there was always trouble. It would start with Granny May talking nasty to him, saying mean things, then he would drink and then he would come for me.

Tessa helped me up the three steps to the front door of the house. She had a large swelling on the side of her face and I knew there had been a fight while I was in the hospital. When they had taken me to the Port Shepstone hospital everything had been neat and tidy. Now the remains of a fight were everywhere. Two of the chairs in the kitchen were broken. Few of the plates and cups had escaped Basil's drunken fury. Once again he had cracked under May's relentless pressure.

I stood in the kitchen imagining the scene, certain from many others that I had witnessed, of what had gone on. May niggling and nagging at Basil. Basil storming out of the house and into the nearest bar. Then coming home full of false confidence. Tessa trying to make the peace as she always did. Basil grabbing someone to hit and Tessa hitting him over the head to try and subdue him. Always the same, Basil coming home drunk and someone getting hurt. After that it was always my turn.

Granny May caught hold of my hand. "It's off to bed with you, young lady. You're not well enough to be up. I can't afford to repeat this little episode."

"No, Mom. Let Debbie sleep with her daddy tonight. Tessa can go back to the hotel alone. Her daddy will look after his ickle-shitty baby."

May let go of my hand and pushed me to my father. "It's about time you took on some of the responsibility. Pity the only time you act like a father is when you're dead drunk."

And so that night Andy and May went to sleep in their room, each with their usual sleeping tablet, and Basil took me to sleep on the truckle bed in the lounge.

He lay beside me smoking a cigarette, the smoke tendrils curling up in a wavering spiral. A bottle of cheap wine stood, half empty, on the coffee table. I watched his face, knowing what was coming.

"Things are really, really bad, my baby."

"I'll make it right, Daddy, I truly will."

"No, you can't, dammit. I'm just a fuck-up."

"No, Dad, no. I love you. You're not."

"I try, baby, I try so hard, but since your mother left I'm useless ..."*

"It's all right, Daddy. I know." I, of all people, knew. Nothing had ever been right since my mother left. She was to blame, of course. Somebody had to take the blame. My father was a victim, but it wasn't his fault. In turn I was his victim, but then I deserved it. Granny May was always on at him and then he would be angry with me. I felt a great wave of despair over me. If I wasn't around everything would be fine for my family.

"At least I have you, baby. You can help me. You're the only good thing in my life. You make it all right for me, don't you, baby."

"Daddy, I'll try."

"It's your fault that Mummy left, you know that, don't you. My side began to hurt but he held me and I couldn't move.

"And your mother isn't here with me. She ran away and left me, the bitch."

"Don't cry, Daddy. I'll find her and bring her back to you. I promise."

"No, you won't. She's gone and won't ever come back. All I've got is you. You make it nice for me, don't you, baby."

Basil rolled over toward me. He started to kiss me. He pushed his tongue into my mouth, so deep that I gagged. His hands pulled at my pyjamas. My breasts were beginning to form, just small roundels of delicate flesh. He began to suck them and squeeze them.

Don't scream, Debbie, I thought, you'll upset Granny, don't scream. Just go away to your safe place. The place inside where no one can touch you. Just endure the pain and the sucking and the spit. It'll be over soon. Make Daddy happy then he won't get upset with Gran. Then Gran won't make him angry and then, and then, round and round trying to make it all right for everybody.

"No, no, please Daddy, no," I whispered.

---

*Negative self-image plays a major role in child abuse, spouse abuse, divorce, crimes ... virtually all failures of humanity.

The physician within, by Catherine Feste, p. 15.

His spit never dried. He needed to lick and suck. He was sucking the life out of me. Soon there would be nothing left. Please, God, just blow me away like the sand on the beach. Please.

When it was over he took me to the bathroom to wash me. I was crying with the pain inside, where that thing had pushed against the cut the doctors made. Once again I had crept away to my safe place where no one could touch me. He hurt me because I deserved it. I was a bad girl and that's what happens to bad girls. It was like a hiding, a different sort of hiding. He tried to wash away the blood and semen, lifting my legs to see where I was hurt. This was not Daddy, this was a horrible thing from the dark, a stranger.

Andy's health continued to deteriorate. In spite of the ministrations of Josiah and myself he became more faltering and frail. When we had been in Munster for about eight months Andy had another small stroke and it was decided that we would move to Margate where there was a doctor and a small clinic should the worst happen.

No sooner had we settled into the small holiday cottage in Margate than Andy died. He slipped away quietly one evening as we were eating our supper. May was devastated. She carried him to her bed and while we waited for the mortuary van she undressed and washed his body. I was taken into the bedroom to watch her sad ministrations and when she had finished she said, "Now, Debbie, give your grandfather a hug and a kiss goodbye." She watched me as I kissed his cooling cheek and then rubbed my lips with the hem of my dress. Then the funeral people came and took him away.

With him went an essential part of May's life. While Andy was alive she had complete control over our lives. She knew just how far she could push him but still she ran things pretty much according to her own vague standards. She had never listened to his advice concerning her children. She had demeaned him and pursued her own path. Yet she wrote in her scrapbook, "Today my beloved husband passed away and the best part of me went with him."

We were now truly without an anchor. May had nothing. Her singing career was over and Andy was dead. Tessa and I were only burdens. Basil was gone again, heaven knows where. Now it was only a matter of waiting for the end.

Chapter 7

From Margate May and I moved to Durban, where Tess joined us. We rented the top story of a large house in Berea. The owner was Barry Shepherd and he lived alone in the bottom half of the house amongst numerous pot plants and books, with a large grey and white cat. I went to school close by and this time I was truly happy. It was an all-girls school and for the first time I felt safe and unthreatened by the presence of males. I made no special friends — I think that the degradation and the humiliation I had suffered at the hands of my father and grandmother isolated me from the normal friendships of childhood. Looking back, I must also have been separated from the ordinary, safe lives of my peers by the vast gap between my sexual experience and their wholesome innocence. But there were other compensations. I discovered something I was good at. I could run. It gave me a sense of purpose and every afternoon I would stay at school and train on the lush green track. I would run and run and run, feel the past drain away, run to something new and fresh. There was a wonderful feeling of exhilaration in losing myself through the breathless effort of pushing my body just a little further. I would come off the track feeling, at last, that I had accomplished something worthwhile. After training I would go to the botanical gardens which were close by. There the solitude and peace began to reconstruct my bruised body and spirit. I would sit for hours alone on a bench in the sun absorbing the tranquillity and serenity.

At first, everything was normal. Basil was not around and I was just another ten year old girl at school, doing the things kids did: homework, athletics, helping out at home. But it didn't last.

May's deterioration was marked. All her life she had relied heavily on pills: pills to sleep, pill to wake her up, pills for blood pressure, on and on. But now in those twilight years her pill bottles begot more pill bottles. They overflowed off the bedside table and onto the floor and I would have to marshal their potent contents in coloured rows for her to take during the day when I was at school. When I left for school she was always still in bed and often would not get up at all. I would come home in the afternoon and find her, slack and pathetic, in a heap on the bed. She had no job or anything else to hold her interest. Tessa was there — but Tessa was, as always, inconspicuous and helpless. May had always depended on me to be there to do all the menial chores. Since the onset of memory I had been there in the shadows of our family life waiting to be called to wash the dishes, make the tea, make my bed, Debbie, Debbie, why aren't you doing what I told you, Debbie, you lazy little slut, I told you ...

In Durban my chores were numerous and humiliating but not unexpected. In the morning she would insist that I clean her false teeth and fit them into her mouth. Then I would have to take the large enamelled chamber pot from under her bed and empty it in the toilet. It would have to be washed to her satisfaction before I could escape to school. There were usually the supper dishes to wash, either in the evening or before I went to school. Once a week I had to cut and file her toenails. These chores were tolerable now that I had a school life, although I was still lonely and separated from other children by my abnormal experiences.

One afternoon I saw that Barry Shepherd had come down to the school grounds. He sat in the grandstand watching me run. Afterwards he walked home with me talking about running and praising my style and speed. From then on he would often be at the track and I felt a sense of comfort that this grandfatherly figure was taking an interest in me. I missed Andy and the stability he had brought to our lives. Barry seemed a good substitute.

Halfway through the athletics season Barry came to our section of the house. "Mrs Reynolds, I've been watching Debbie. She's a fine athlete with lots of potential, and I'd like to train her."

Granny May was flattered. Here at last was something the child could do. And do well, by all accounts. Of course she agreed to Barry's suggestion. From then on Barry would be at the track every afternoon, helping, advising, rubbing my aching legs, just being there. When I finished training he would put an arm round me and give me a quick hug. Then a kiss. Then the hugs and the kisses stretched out.

My father's despicable training kicked in. He had trained me to be aware of every nuance and every shade of sexual advance and I realised that this man wanted more than I should have been prepared to give him. At that time, sex meant Basil and not any other man. There had only been Basil. Basil had not yet sold me to other men — and, in any event, I trusted Barry, so I was confused between my advanced knowledge of sexuality and my longing to have a sincere and safe father-figure in my life. Since the age of six I had had confusing messages about the role of sex and love from Basil, so I suppose it was not unusual for me to feel bewildered by the sexual signals emanating from this other man.

Over the weeks I grew more and more uncomfortable with his nearness. His stealthy touches were like slime on my skin and when his pale blue eyes narrowed as he looked at my body I knew exactly what he wanted.

After Barry started to train me Granny May quickly began to take advantage of the situation. She would send me down to Barry's half of the house demanding that he fix this or change that. Or she would stand at the top of the stairs and scream for Barry to come up and do something. This began to rile Barry, especially when he had friends in his apartment. I felt deeply humiliated as her demands grew ever more strident.

Then Granny May stopped paying the rent. Neither she nor Tessa were working. She reasoned that her widow's pension wasn't enough to support the three of us. She began pleading poverty to Barry, pleading that this child was such a drain, such a burden. I could feel his anger building up. When he began to say, "I've had enough of this woman," it looked as if we were going to have to move again. I feared that all the special things in my life were going to be lost one more time. The school, my athletics, the botanical gardens.

Looking back, I wonder if my need for the stability of those normal things was so great that I precipitated the events that followed. Even at ten years old I had become wise in sexual matters. Perhaps I did egg him on because I knew exactly what he wanted, and I knew with certainty that if I played my cards right we would get to stay in the house and I could continue to go to the school where, at last, I was so happy. And it didn't take very much. One day he asked if he could kiss me and I said yes. Then he pushed me onto his bed. I remember the smell of dust, the paisley bedspread and a picture of Tretchikoff's weeping rose on the wall.

"If you let me do this then I won't tell your Gran to leave." This was exactly what I wanted to hear and I allowed him to paw at my breasts and then penetrate me. It wasn't difficult for me to please him, Basil had taught me well. But I was dead, my holy inner self in some distant land where it was safe, only my body visible and busy.

It was at this stage that I started using other people for my own gain. I found I could extract promises or get things that ordinarily I couldn't have. I discovered that in the world of the paedophile there are always rewards, always something the child needs. In this case I gained a roof over our heads.

But the price was going to get higher yet. Barry was a very sociable person. He had a number of friends who would get together in his rooms, drinking and talking and playing records. On each occasion he would call me down on some pretext or the other. I wasn't sure what this was all about until one day he had confronted me with one of his friends. He said that he had told this man what we were doing together — and the man wanted to do it as well.

"It'll be OK if he does it with you. I'll be here and I'll watch that he does-n't hurt you. Besides, you like living here, don't you?"

And so I let the other man do what he wanted while Barry watched and masturbated hungrily. Once I had allowed one other man while Barry was watching it became easier for him to invite two men or a group to watch. While one man was penetrating me another would be kissing me and still another fondling my budding breasts. No one was allowed to enter me until Barry had done so. He owned me and he was the initiator. After that anybody could use me in whatever way they chose. Objects were used, bot-tles, vibrators, anything.*

Then one day someone produced a movie camera — and that was my introduction to the sordid world of child pornography. These men were paedophiles. Always very gentle and sweet, sickly sweet with soft skin and insidiously soft, wet lips. Never strong men, always wimpish, soft men with no hair on their bodies. Like slugs. Foul, disgusting. Sometimes there would be women there, watching, drinking, enjoying the spectacle of a child being abused. Sometimes up to five or six or more men at a time, and I would have to accommodate them all. By this stage I was so deeply involved that to get out of it without the help of some caring adult would have been impossible.

In the end, after about a year, we moved from Durban after all. And I was left wondering what was the point of all I had had to endure, all I had been forced to do. It had all been for nothing.

---

*How do [these children] act when they are with a group of men molesting them? Truthfully they are manipulated psychologically to such a degree that their facial expres-sions are blank, as though they were thinking: Just get it over with ... They are over-whelmed with shame much of the time and simply comply with the wishes of the adult.
A paedophile quoted in Child pornography, by Tim Tate, p. 10.

Chapter 8

The return to Johannesburg was ignominious. We stayed in one sleazy, decrepit boarding house after another, each one for a few months at a time, and then when May had sufficiently antagonised everyone, we would pack our suitcases and move to another even more seedy place. With Andy's death my grandmother had lost her sense of purpose. She gave up singing entirely and with that it seemed as if life had begun to slip from her grasp. She had had no opportunities to sing since Andy died and now there seemed little to sing about.

In spite of Andy's shadowy role in our lives he had at least given May direction and purpose, now we drifted without rudder or anchor. I began to learn that I could buy what I wanted with my eleven year old body and there were many men who were happy to pay the small amount of money I asked in return for my favours. I had learned all the sexual tricks I needed. Basil and then Basement Barry had been thorough if uncaring teachers and I an able but reluctant pupil.*

For me and those who used me sex was not the romantic "moon/June" affair of normal people. Sex was allowing groping strangers their few moments of release in some dark urine-stained stairwell or on a musty unmade bed. Sex was allowing men and sometimes women to knead my still half-formed breasts with their rough hands and push strange things into my body. Sex was photographs taken and movies filmed while I lay passive and unseeing. In those moments I continued to find my core self slipping away into some protected haven while my body was being abased and abused. This was the only way I could follow the path that Basil had set me on and still remain untouched. No man who used me could have

---

*Children's minds are like tape recorders. They absorb what they see and hear and tend to believe indiscriminately all the messages to which they are exposed.
The physician within, by Catherine Feste, p. 19.

guessed that when he did what he had to do he was using an untenanted body while the real me flew free from his contamination.

I used to wonder sometimes how I survived, but I realise now that it was instinctive. How do other kids live through this sort of thing? It wasn't that I wanted to go on living, I just did. One day simply followed the next. I had only strength enough to live one day at a time. And it was all so secret. I never told anyone. Firstly, there was no one in my life to tell and secondly I was so filled with guilt and shame and fear that I dared not tell. And so this sordid thing grew and was sustained in my secret world.

Finally, tired of wandering around the ragged edges of Johannesburg, May decided to move back to Kenilworth and we found accommodation in a tarnished little hotel very near to Great Britain Street. We had a room on the first floor reached by a set of narrow mouldy stairs. By this time May was extremely fat and ungainly and she would have to call on the men in the bar to help heave her upstairs. Once inside the room she'd kick off her underwear, flop on the bed and call me to come and wash her. "C'mon, Debbie, bring a rag and wash me." With her fat legs wide open she would open her podgy pudenda still further with her fingers. "You never cleaned it properly. Do it again."

It was at this time that I allowed myself to acknowledge my intense hatred of my grandmother. But even that emotion was so foreign to me that I needed to punish myself for feeling anything at all. I got back at her by slipping out at night and prostituting myself to the men who stood around drinking in the bar. It was never difficult, there was always someone there who wanted a quick fuck and who was happy to pay fifty cents or a rand for the pleasure.

One day, May decided that I was too much trouble and enrolled me in a boarding school out of town. For two months I lived the normal life of a carefree child, with classes in the morning, sport in the afternoon and safety and security when I went to bed. Then she decided that she couldn't do without me and I went back with her to the old life of scrubbing her teeth, emptying her chamber pot, cutting her ever-hardening toenails and fucking the men in the bar.

I was enrolled in the Park Junior School and for a while life settled into an illusion of a routine. My work at school had never been good. Each termend my report cards mirrored the same dreary comments, "Debbie could do better", "Debbie doesn't apply herself", "Debbie spends too much time dreaming". I recognise now that there were many clues signalling an abused child but in the late sixties and early seventies these were neither recognised nor understood. Teachers and other professionals had not been trained to pick up signals such as I had been sending all my life and I was too afraid, too guilty, to tell. Many may have suspected, and I still bear deep resentment towards those adults who have since told me that they thought "something" was going on but did nothing to help me. Those people were passive perpetrators, and share in the guilt of those who abused me.

Then came a momentous change in my circumstances. At the beginning of the second term at Park Junior I was moved into another class. On the first morning my new teacher walked into the classroom and with that my life changed forever, for it was not the young teacher I saw but an angel in a blue and cream dress. I could almost see the outline of shimmering wings and a golden halo round her dark hair as she moved around the classroom speaking softly to her charges. She came to me and placed her hand on my shoulder and smiled down at me and I knew that I was looking up into the face of my ideal person. This was the person I wanted to grow up to be like. I wanted to have her dark swinging hair and her eyes that crinkled in the corners from many smiles. Above all I wanted, like her, to be innocent of shame and guilt and ugliness. The angel's name was Ruth Nielsen.

Miss Nielsen noticed me, saw something in me that was worthy of concern and began to make a special effort to give me the sense of self-esteem that I lacked. She put me in charge of various facets of classroom life, the stationery cupboard and the class register, and paid attention to me in other small ways. I began to be somebody in the classroom and with a growing confidence my attitude to school work changed. I began to score Cs and then Bs and, finally, As in my work. At times I would go to school in terrible pain, for Basil had reappeared on the scene and many times he used me so often in the night that I would not be able to sit the next day. Never once did I venture to tell Ruth of my home life. I was afraid that I would be blamed, afraid that Granny May would be blamed, afraid that my father would go to prison. I had no sense that I mattered, nor was there any thought of what I wanted for myself or that I had rights as a child. I was too busy protecting everybody else in my life to understand that the first and most important person to protect was myself. I even protected Ruth, for I didn't want her to know what a "bad" person I was and what ugly things I did. If only I had had the courage to tell somebody then, what a different life I would have had, but my secret stayed locked within me until it was forced from me many years later.

When I started to get distinctions for my work the principal of the school wondered if Miss Nielsen was favouring me and giving me credits for which I hadn't worked. She moved me from Ruth's class to another but still I thrived and the atmosphere of loving acceptance continued. My grandmother soon noticed the changes in me and suspected that Ruth had something to do with them. She developed a passionate hatred for my mentor and tried to cast her in a bad light but her disparaging comments had no impact on me. The intensity of her hatred grew as though she saw in Ruth a rival for control over me. If I walked with Ruth to the bus stop after school I knew that I would get a severe beating with a wire coathanger from May when I got back to the hotel. If I spoke Ruth's name May would slap my face for mentioning her in the house. But at last I had a comparison. I knew how things could be and although this intensified the pain of things as they were, I became a considerably happier child.

I still lived in a world where perverted sex predominated. Basil was always on the periphery, coming and going as his mean life ebbed and flowed. I was still selling myself in that dingy little hotel bar to whoever wanted me. Among the men who spent their afternoons lounging in the squalid and smoky bar was an uncle of mine. He made an arrangement with me that every Thursday afternoon, when his wife went to have her hair done, I would walk the few blocks to his house and there sell myself to him for fifty cents. His needs were simple, he was quick, and with the proceeds I was able to pay for guitar lessons with my beloved Ruth.

May's sister, Caroline, lived close enough for us to visit. Her large dank house was not far from our old place in Great Britain Street and May would drag me there every few weeks for a lengthy visit. I don't remember ever seeing Caroline's legs; to my knowledge she never walked, but spent her days in bed with the dusty venetian blinds closed and a bucket near the bed so that she spared herself even the short walk to the toilet. While there was a great deal of tension between May and Caroline, I think that they drew sustenance from each other as the matriarchs of their respective families. Whenever we called May and Caroline would drink tea and gossip in the bedroom. If I stayed around too long May would call out, "Don't sit around here counting teeth. Get outside and play."

And so I was left to entertain myself, to wander around, a ready victim for any sort of mischief. The grounds were sprawling, with a swimming pool near the bottom and beyond that a dense shrubbery. One day there was a sharp hiss from under the shrubbery and as I got closer I noticed that a girl about my age was sitting there with a large dog. Her name was Angela and she lived next door. Soon I got to know her and her brother and I suppose it was natural that when I went to Caroline's house I gravitated to these two who would come and collect me to "play" with them while the old ladies gossiped over tea and biscuits. Bertie was about thirteen years old, a large boy with loose lips and corn coloured hair. He enjoyed holding me down with his knees on my arms and his hands flitting over my breasts while the black gardener held my legs aloft and raped me. Angela had a penchant for animals and would expect me to be an admiring voyeur while she enjoyed sex with their German Shepherd, the two of us well hidden in the thick shrubbery in Aunt Caroline's garden.

I wonder now why my small world was so peopled with dysfunctional human beings. Looking back I recognise that there was no one whose life was solid and stable. I don't remember initiating many of my sexual experiences, but I understand now that an abused person always feels that they have a large sticker on the forehead stating "I'm in for sex". It goes with the territory. What was I doing that gave people permission to do those kinds of things to me? Becoming sexually aware at such an early age must have changed me in ways that were too veiled and too covert for me to understand even now. Once I had become sexually experienced all it took was to come into contact with an abuser or a potential abuser and a subtle contract was made.

My grandmother never once came to look for me, to see if I was all right. I could have been face down in the swimming pool and she would have continued drinking tea and gossiping with Caroline. I was just a lonely little girl wandering alone in a seedy world with the unrealistic belief that I was there to be responsible for all my family.

One incident at that time ensured that I would remain indelibly locked into the belief that I was there to protect everyone. One evening Basil took me for a ride in his car. Granny May was always happy to see her son paying attention to me, little realising what that "attention" entailed.

"Mom, I'm just going to take Debbie out for a while," Basil said.

"That's good, Basil, but don't drink while you've got Debbie with you."

Basil's reaction was typical, "Of course not, Mom, don't you have any faith in me?"

Basil often took me out in his car and then he would park in some side street and rape me. I thought this occasion would be no different. This particular evening he was in a foul mood. The night before he had been badly beaten up in a pub brawl and May had told him to stop drinking ... or else. He was foul mouthed as he pushed me into the front seat of the car and drove me to a squalid hotel in Mayfair. There was a dark lane up the side of the building that led to a shebeen where black people were able to drink and dance. Shebeens were illegal in those days but the police tended to turn a blind eye to the noisy revelry, provided it remained within the walls of the shebeen. Basil parked in this fetid lane and left me in the car while he went into the bar. It seemed hours before he and another man came back and I spent the time crouched in the back fearfully clutching a small pocket knife I had found on the floor of the car while curious people stopped, peered into the car and then walked away.

"Daddy, I'm scared. Please take me home," I whined.

"Shit, Debbie, don't you ever want to be with your father?"

"Daddy, please, I'm scared."

"You lousy little bastard. You never want to be with me. You're always bloody whining. Just shut the fuck up, will you."

The two men stood talking for a while, passing a bottle between them, and

I heard them laugh. Then Basil pulled me from the car and I thought that he was going to push me down and hold me for his friend. But Basil had other ideas. He and the other man stood around for some while, laughing and talking idly. Then a young black woman came out of the shebeen and walked towards them. Basil grabbed her and threw her down on the ground. She was crying, "No, baas. No, baas," as he tore off her clothes and thrust strongly into her. He kept looking at me as if this was a lesson he was going to teach me. The other man held my arms down at my sides and fondled and touched me as he watched Basil.

"You see what I'll do to other women if you don't let me, Debbie."

I remember a numbness. There was nothing I could do to help this weeping woman.

"Watch, Debbie, watch how hard I'm doing her. You can stop this happening, Debbie."

Trying to stop Basil would have resulted in a beating and rape for both the woman and myself. I stood still.

"You let me do it to you, Debbie, and I won't do this to other women. See, Debbie, see what I'm doing to her. See how nice it is."

I closed my mind to what was happening, knowing that I would continue allowing my father to rape me if it meant that I would be protecting other women. I wished that I could help her but I went on silently watching, knowing that there was nothing I could do.

That night as on so many other occasions I hated the man he became with such intensity that I wished him painfully dead.

What carried me sky high through those days and nights was the absolute belief that one day I would be like Ruth, that I would be someone special and do something good in the world. She didn't have to be a saint or a perfect being to be an example to me, just to show me a pattern of what I could become. Ruth showed me a different kind of life, that things could be different for me. One day she invited me to go with her to Sunday School and it wasn't long before I was going with her every week. In the early days Granny May used to go to church and enjoyed singing in the choir or at weddings, largely because of the admiration from other choir members for her voice. I used to be given a couple of cents on a Sunday and dressed to go to Sunday School, but I would spend the money at the local café and sit outside on the pavement until it was time to go home. As a result I didn't know much about religion or spiritual things. But Ruth changed all that.

One day after Sunday School Ruth took me back to her home for tea and cake. "Debbie," she said, "you can give your heart to the Lord and he will forgive you, whatever it is, he will forgive you and he will wash away your sins."

I sat for a long while on the carpet at Ruth's feet. Forgive me? I thought. You're crazy. You don't know the half of it, Ruth. I'm not worthy of God's love or attention. All the years I had prayed for him to protect me and to stop what was happening and it still went on. Didn't that show he was uncaring? Then it occurred to me that Ruth was right, had to be right for anything to make sense, and at that moment I truly believed that maybe, just maybe, God would set things straight in my life. Maybe he would wipe away all my sins and I would be problem-free from then on. I put my teacup down very carefully and got onto my knees. With my beloved Ruth holding my hands, I prayed to God to forgive me and set me free. From that moment on, through all I was still to endure, my faith in an ever-loving and forgiving God was often challenged but never diminished.

About this time Basil lost his job and didn't seem to have either the energy or will to look for another one. He lounged around in the room, listless and complaining. Each week May would dole out a few rands for "pocket money" and his ego would be even further deflated. There were times when he disappeared and we would get word that he was again living on the streets. Finally he came back to stay, and with a scheme more devilish than any before.

One Friday night he told May that he was taking me to watch the local soccer team practise in the park. May thought it a good idea. "Both of you need to get out and get some fresh air," she said.

It was winter, and dark when we got to the park. Basil led me to the men's toilets on the side of the field. There was a bunch of lounging men joking and laughing, about ten or eleven of them, all in soccer kit. Basil sat outside smoking while the men led me into the toilet. One by one they had sex with me, some lying me down, some forcing me to bend over so they could enter me from the back, some making me stand on the toilet so they could watch each other. One had a movie camera and through my blank eyes I watched as he positioned himself for the best shots. When it was over they went outside and paid Basil. I walked out after them.

"It's over, Daddy, we can go home now."

This became a Friday night ritual, one from which I could not escape, not even in my sleep.

It was about this time that I started menstruating. I was used to bleeding; every time I had sex or was penetrated by an object I bled, so when I started my first menstrual cycle I was not shocked by this new turn of events. I remember going to my grandmother and explaining that I was starting my "monthlies". May was ecstatic. She ran to the telephone and called the local chemist. "Mr Sauer, my granddaughter, Debbie, has just started her monthlies. I'm sending her down to your shop, so you get everything she needs ready for her. She'll come now and collect it."

"Debbie," she said, "go down to the chemist. He knows why you're coming. He'll give you pads and everything."

"You told him?"

"Of course, just go, you stupid child. Mr Sauer's waiting for you."

The visit to the chemist was almost beyond humiliation, although the man was as kind as he could be. When I got back to the hotel May had a few of the other guests in our room, telling them that her granddaughter was now a "woman".

I graduated from Park Junior School with distinction and went to Sir John Adamson High School. Ruth remained a teacher in the junior school and, while I didn't entirely lose contact with her, I felt very much cast adrift. Granny May and I left the hotel and moved into a small flat in the same street. Things got very bad at home, as Basil was there most of the time and I had to endure his demands during the day when Granny May was out as well as in the nights when she would take her sleeping tablets and sleep soundly through it all.

It was at this time that I began to feel the first stirrings of adolescent love. Jamie was in my class and he would share his sandwiches with me and joke and laugh with me at break times. Eventually he came to the flat to see me and one hot summer evening we sat on the small balcony overlooking the park, awkward and new at this attraction. Gingerly, he edged his arm around my waist and bent over to kiss me.

There was an explosion of movement behind us. May burst onto the balcony and grabbed hold of me. She brought her hand up and slapped my face. I felt the warm drip of blood onto my blouse. "You little bitch! I know what you're up to out there. I won't have you whoring around in my house. Do you hear me? There'll be no nonsense while I'm around."

The situation rapidly became more than I could handle. Each day held its own horror and even my sleep had begun to be infested by my experiences. Terrible nightmares would wake me screaming and thrashing in a sweat-soaked bed, nightmares so bad that I feared closing my eyes in case I should be sucked into the abyss of my deeds. The dreams were peopled by all the men who had handled me since I was six years old and by their snatching hands and wet lips. In my dreams I relived every rape, every clutch, every foul deed, over and over and over again. My desperation and anger knew no bounds; my father and grandmother each abusing me in their own fashion, no one to speak to, no one who knew the extent of my deteriorating psyche. One day in a fit of anger I caught a small cockroach and set it alight, watching with grim satisfaction as it writhed and squirmed and finally died.

In desperation I ran away from my grandmother's home and found my way to Ruth. She was right, of course; I couldn't run from it, and so she sent me back. I ran away again and went to Jenny. She allowed me to stay but I was bombarded by the guilt of having "done" something terrible to Gran, after all she had done for me. It was then that Jenny dropped her bombshell. "Wouldn't you like to know where Mommy is?" she said.

"What? You know where she's living?" I was shaken.

"Of course," Jenny smiled. "I've known all along. We've been writing to each other for years."

As soon as I realised I could be in contact with my mother a terrible need arose in me to know her, to be with her and to feel her warm mother's arms around me. Here at last was a solution to all my problems. My mother would be the one to take me away from all I had been suffering; she would rescue me. She would be a good person; she couldn't be like my grandmother's family. No one could be as bad as them.

I formed a desperate desire to go to her but May would not hear of it. "She's in America, you stupid girl. I'm not letting you go. Who knows what will happen to you there. Besides, you belong to me now and I refuse to allow such nonsense."

At this time I became very involved with the church's youth group. Here I had a modicum of freedom and could sing and joke and be an ordinary teenager. I had friends in the group and they cared about me in a way that I had never before experienced. But the nightmares had reached such proportions that I was afraid to sleep. I would read until all hours of the night. I would lie in bed holding my eyelids open in a vain attempt to stay awake. Inevitably exhaustion would claim me and I would wake again and again moaning and sick with anguish. One night at a youth group meeting I collapsed with exhaustion. They rushed me to the South Rand Hospital but the doctors were too busy to care and it was easy for them to hand me packets of sleeping pills and tranquillisers. After a few months I had several packets of them, pink ones, yellow ones, and green and white capsules, at least seven different kinds all shoved into the back of a drawer in the house.

One day I took the tablets out and stared at them and realised that they represented a way out. If I took enough of them I could scare May into letting me go to my mother in America. What a brilliant idea! That'll shock them, I thought, that'll teach them. They'll know just how desperate I am and they'll let me go. I walked to the kitchen with a handful of pills and swallowed them down with a glass of water. Before I had got to the kitchen door something weird began to happen to my legs. I slumped to the floor and the world slipped quietly away from me.

I woke up in the intensive care ward at the hospital. There were pipes and tubes coming out of me everywhere and through the blurred light I could see Ruth and her mother standing at the edge of my vision. They were crying. Apparently I had been calling for Ruth and as the doctors felt that I wouldn't survive, she was allowed to stay with me and hold my hand while we waited for my death.

Still later May and Basil arrived.

"Debbie, please don't die. Debbie, how could you have done this to us." May was distraught.

A few days later she dropped the bombshell: "Jenny's been in touch with your mother. She's sending you a plane ticket and you can go to America."

I was about to be rescued.

Chapter 9

In January 1973, three months before I turned thirteen, I left South Africa — for good, I thought — to start a new life with my mother in America. It was a terrifying beginning. I had never flown in an aeroplane before, but even more alarming was that I didn't even know what my mother looked like or whether I would be recognised at the airport. All I knew was that she wanted me and she was going to make everything right for me.

I suppose I was pretty emotionally unstable at that time. I was two months out of a serious suicide attempt and still the victim of horrifying nightmares. But I knew with the complete certainty that only the very young can possess that I had come to the end of the bad parts of my life and that my mother was my rescuer and saviour. Nothing was ever going to hurt me again, she would see to that. God had answered my prayers at last.

The trip to Heathrow Airport from Johannesburg was tiring but uneventful. I told anyone who had patience to listen that I was going to live with my mother in America. I was joyous with anticipation. There was to be a three hour stop-over in Heathrow, but I was in for a shock. There had been a delay and I would have to wait for 36 hours before going on to New York. No one had thought to book me into a hotel or even to make sure that I had a meal in those long hours. I was too frightened to get myself a cup of coffee because I didn't know how the coffee machine worked. I was too frightened to ask for help, too frightened even to sleep. I spent the 36 hours huddled in a chair wondering what was going to happen to me. I must have been a pathetic sight, a young girl huddled in a corner in jeans, T-shirt and sandals, incongruous among the seasoned and sophisticated travellers. I kept my eyes lowered in case I caught the glance of some sympathetic person, for this would surely have reduced me to the tears that were so near the surface.

At JFK Airport in New York people were more kindly and directed me onto the bus that would take me to the internal flights terminal. Then on to Los

Angeles. The closer I got to Los Angeles the closer I was to utter fright. What if my mother wasn't there to meet me? What if I didn't recognise her or she me? I was relying on a sort of psychic moment when mother and child would link eyes and just know each other, but would that happen? What was it going to be like? And what would she be like?

Riding the escalator at Los Angeles Airport, I scanned the crowd of people waiting to greet us, wondering which of the happily waving women was my mother. Then a tall man came towards me. "Debbie? I'm Dell, your father." He wrapped his arms around me and gave me a tight hug. "Welcome to America."

"But where's my mother?"

There was a slight pause. I was sensitive at interpreting pauses, and felt a twinge of premonition. "She's waiting for you in San Diego. We have to catch another plane and she'll be there."

We sat side by side on the last leg of my journey and talked and talked. Dell was full of questions about my journey and I was full of questions about my new home. He told me about his job at the San Diego Zoo and about their nine year old son, Howard. He told me that they had applied for me to go to the local school but had waited for me to arrive before making final arrangements. He told me that I had my own room and that they had carefully chosen pastel colours for the wallpaper and curtains. He hoped I would like the colours. Of course I would. Of course. There was an instant rapport. This was my new father and he cared about me even from the first moment. Things were going to be all right, after all.

At the San Diego airport my mother still didn't appear, but Dell didn't seem too perturbed and I imagined that I had misunderstood him. On the way to their house I began to wonder what he would want of me. What was the price I would have to pay for all this? Were all fathers like Basil? Would he want what Basil had demanded of me? Somehow I thought not, but I couldn't be sure.

We drove to a little house with a short white picket fence. Dell pulled into the driveway. For a moment he sat still then he took hold of my hand and began patting it clumsily. "Honey, it's good to have you here. I've always wanted a daughter and now I got one all ready made. It's going to work out, I know it is. Just give her a chance, will you?" There were tears in his eyes.

Inside, the living room was filled with people. A large banner proclaiming Welcome Home, Debbie hung across a corner and people pressed from all sides to hug me and make me feel at home. There was a huge cake on a table loaded with good things to eat and in the corner a stuffed kangaroo with a label round its neck that proclaimed "To Debbie with love from Dell". I looked at all the smiling faces. Which of these women was my mother? Then the crowd parted and a small woman weaved towards me. She had short dark hair, glasses and a dumpy figure. Her face was lined and old. There was a glass of something dark in her hand.

"So, you're Debbie." She stood looking at me. "You look just like your fucking father."

These were the first words my mother said to me. No answering words came but I felt an almost overmastering urge to get down on my knees in front of her and beg her to love me. I put my arms round her to give her a hug and she smelled of liquor. Somewhere deep inside I began to doubt whether this was going to work. Over my mother's shoulder I caught a glimpse of Dell. There was a strained smile on his face. She's not supposed to be like this, I thought, overwhelmed with a familiar pain. She's supposed to be better than the people I left back home.

Life settled into an uneasy routine. I had my own room and new clothes. Myra took me to an eye specialist and instead of the dark-framed spectacles which I normally wore, I was fitted with contact lenses. I was not too sure about this, because looking as dowdy and as ugly as possible had always been my way of protecting myself from unwanted attention. Not that it had helped — but I still wasn't sure that I wanted to look pretty. I went to the local school and immediately fell in love with the sense of freedom and energy there.

Since Dell had left the Navy and worked as a chef at the San Diego Zoo he had fairly regular hours. He was always home in the evenings and this brought a semblance of stability to our lives. Myra did not work outside the home but took her duties as a housewife very seriously. She cooked to perfection and the house was always immaculate but at two o'clock each afternoon, when her chores were done, she would sit down in the living room with a bottle of bourbon and get solidly plastered. By the time her husband came home she was normally paralytic. Then, not trusting her legs, she would scream for him to take her to bed. Dell would gently pick her up and carry her like a small child to bed and to sleep.

When Myra was sober we had a good relationship. When she was drunk she became verbally abusive and filled with hatred for me, for herself for abandoning her children, for my father who could not make the choice between his wife and his mother, and especially for May Reynolds. And I bore the brunt of her loathing. In her worst moments she told me how worthless I was and how glad she was that she had left me. She blamed me for the break-up of her marriage to Basil and told me that it was time I went back "to where I belonged". From the periphery of the developing chaos Dell looked on with a baffled sense of helplessness. This wasn't how it was meant to be. Myra had always spoken of me with such love and longing, but now that seemed to have been washed away by the ever-increasing tide of bourbon.

Looking back, I wonder if I didn't provoke her in some way. After all the events in my life where alcohol had played such a destructive part, I couldn't tolerate the smell or the taste of liquor. When my mother was sober I loved her but when she was drunk I hated and despised her. She may have suspected that and reacted accordingly. Once again, I was jeopardising a relationship that should have survived because I could not speak of what had happened to me.

Dell was wonderful, and tried to make up for Myra in little ways. He took me to the stores and bought me clothes and shoes. He took Howard and me to the movies and to the ball park. The stuffed kangaroo that he had given me as a welcoming present stood in the corner of my room as evidence of his love for me.

Howard, my step-brother, was a sad little boy who clung to me from the moment we met. We formed a loving bond, each of us the sad victim of our mother's drunken regrets. I could see that Howard's attachment to me was making Myra angry and jealous, but we both had need of each other and so I ignored the warning signs.

School was a time when I could escape from the atmosphere at home. I continued to do well with my school work and began to form normal friendships with the kids in my class. There was Paddy, a beautiful girl with long black hair who introduced herself to me with a "Hiya, kiddo" on the first day. Paddy came from a dysfunctional home and took drugs. She often tried to persuade me to have a smoke but my answer was always no. I had seen what my father was like when he had smoked that stuff. I had experienced his monstrous behaviour when his mind was clouded and tinged with marijuana and I wasn't going to have even an experimental puff. Besides that I was too busy protecting myself and others, too busy coping, too busy keeping secrets, too busy controlling as far as I could the events in my life to want to be drugged. No ways. That stuff was not for me.

Then there was Neil. Neil was in my class and sat close enough to pass me notes. He fell in love with me and pestered me to elope with him.

"C'mon, Neil. We're still kids. That's just crazy."

"No, it isn't. We could go down to Mexico. It'd be great. Let's do it, Debbie."

When I began to feel that I couldn't deal with my mother's alcoholism any longer I wrote to Ruth telling her what was happening. I was naive enough to give the letter to my mother to post and she opened it and read what I had written.

"How dare you write such lies about me? What right have you got to come here, live in my house and then spread this kind of filth about me?"

"Mom," I began.

"Don't `Mom' me. I never wanted you here. I don't want you now. Just go back to your father where you belong."

"Please don't send me back. Please, Mom. I can't go back."

"Well you're going, because I'm going to get the ticket and put you on the next plane. I don't want you here. I never wanted you in the first place. Get the hell out of my life."

Around about Thanksgiving I developed severe toothache but Myra refused to take me to a dentist. "You can just suffer," she said. Eventually, when I could stand the pain no longer, a neighbour took pity on me and took me to have an abscess lanced and drained.

By Christmas things had got very bad between Myra and myself. She was barely able to speak to me and Dell and Howard were the unhappy buffers between Myra's apparent hatred of me and my anguished silence. Two days before Christmas Dell and Howard and I went to the stores to buy Myra a present. We chose a large oak Welsh dresser, something we knew that she wanted.

When we got home Myra was drunk. She grabbed hold of me, pulled me into the living room and shoved me down into a chair.

"That's the end," she screamed. "You've been fucking my husband and now you're going to get the hell out of my house."

She turned to Dell. "You bastard. Seeing you've been fucking her all along why don't you take her upstairs and do it some more."

With those words my world collapsed. This was the mother who was supposed to rescue me. Was there something about me? Did I have the word "sex" tattooed on my forehead? Was it because I looked like my father or was it that, for Myra, I represented everything she hated about the family? I started to cry and Dell gently told me to go to my room.

"I'm sorry, Mom. I'm so sorry."

Dell gave me a gentle push. "Debs, it's not your fault."

But of course it was. It had always been my fault.

When it looked as if I was going to have to go back to South Africa I fell into a major depression. Nothing shattered me as much as my mother's rejection, not even the first time that Basil raped me. There had been an excuse for my father, I thought, every time he did it I could think of a hundred reasons why. I was "bad", I was the "cause" of all the unhappiness in his life. But Myra had no such excuse. I had done nothing wrong. Everything I did to try to win her love and approval had been in vain.

I phoned Jenny and told her what had happened. "Jenny, please, I want to come back. Please let me come and stay with you."

"Of course, you can stay with me." Jenny's voice was filled with sympathy.

"Jenny, just promise me one thing. Please don't let Granny or my father be there at the airport. Promise me that you won't send me back to live with Granny or Dad. I can't go back to them. Please promise me."

"I promise you. Debs, you can live with me and Jeff."

I felt a bit better knowing that when I got back to South Africa at least I wouldn't have to live in the same horrifying conditions that I had left.

Almost a year after I had arrived in America, so full of hope and optimism, Dell silently drove me back to the airport to return home. My last words to my mother were, "Mom, if you ever need me you know where I'll be." Little did I know that fourteen years later she would remember those words and call me to her once again.

The flight back from America was mostly silent. What could I say to anyone who asked? That my mother had rejected me a second time? At Heathrow I half-formed a plan. If I was to walk out of the airport and into the streets, no one would even miss me. No one would be able to find me and drag me back. But I wasn't street-wise despite all my experiences and I knew with certainty that I would never be able to survive on the back streets of London.

On the plane from London to Johannesburg I sat next to a man who tried to talk to me. I ignored him and tried to pretend that I was all alone on the plane. There was little that I wanted to say to anyone, least of all a strange man. After the lights had been dimmed I saw his hands move and realised he was masturbating, watching me through eyes glazed with intent. Dear God, was there never going to be an end to all this?

At Jan Smuts Airport I collected my luggage, my stuffed kangaroo, the guitar that Dell had given me and walked through the international arrival doors. There outside stood May and my father. Jenny had betrayed me. The one person that I thought I could trust had let me down.

Basil hugged me and Granny May fussed with a handkerchief pressed to her eyes. "There, you see, I told you; your mother didn't really want you. It's just as well that you're back with people who love you."

"Everything's going to be different now, Debs," Basil took my hand. "We're living in Vanderbijlpark now. I've got a good job and things are going to be different. I promise."

At fourteen I suppose there resided in me a well of indestructible optimism. I can remember thinking, well, perhaps things won't be as bad as they were before. It's got to get better. It can't ever be as bad as it had been.

The house in Vanderbijlpark was very ordinary but pleasant. Once again, though, I had to share a room with May while Basil and Tessa slept in the main bedroom. Basil enrolled me in the local high school and for two weeks things were good.

Then one afternoon Basil came home early. He was drunk.

Chapter 10

Basil was more brutal than I remembered. Perhaps it was because I had not had sex for over a year — but, whatever it was, pain and despair ripped through me. This time I found the strength to scream, "No! No! No!" I fought but he was too strong. As he came to a roaring climax the door opened and Tessa stood there. Basil got up and, without a look at either of us, walked to his bedroom and fell asleep. I lay on the floor, my face covered, crying uncontrollably while Tessa stood over me shaking and white. I wish there were words to describe what I felt for him at that moment. Hatred is too mild. Murderous rage is, again, too mild. But a frantic desire to mutilate this foul, evil, inhuman, devilish man began deep inside and threatened to spill over into something which I would not be able to control. How dare you do this to me, you bastard. Never! Never! Never again will you touch me. I'm going to make you pay if it's the last thing I do!

Tessa stood looking at me, speechless at the sight of my humiliation. Then she took some bank notes out of her pocket and thrust them at me.

"Go, Debbie, go now. If you don't they'll kill you. Both of them. I'll cover for you but get out now, while you still can."

I ran for my bike. But where to go? There was nowhere, and no one to help me. Then I remembered Bernie Mullen, my domestic science teacher at Sir John Adamson High School. She had shown that she cared about me and I had built up a rapport with her. I couldn't go to Ruth, who had been so happy for me when I left for America. I felt a deep sense of guilt that I hadn't lived up to her expectations and made a success of life with my mother. But Bernie had not been aware of my failure. She was also the only one I could think of who lived close enough. She was in the southern suburbs of Johannesburg, 55 kilometres away.

I had been raped and I was bleeding. The journey on my bicycle was a nightmare. The saddle chafed and burned into my dreadfully violated parts. Every now and again I would have to get off when the pain got too bad. Every now and then a car would stop and some smirking man would offer me a lift. Each one was refused with the overspill of contempt I was feeling for my father. It must have been near supper time when at last I knocked on Bernie's door. She could not hide her feelings of dismay at seeing me, but she took me in and gave me something to eat and drink. Then she put me in the car and took me back to Gran. I begged her, please don't send me back there, please. At one point I tried to throw myself out of her car, but she held on to me. When May saw me she threw up her hands in mock despair. "I've had enough of this child. No more." Then she turned her back on me and walked into the house.

I packed a suitcase and left with Bernie.

I stayed with Bernie and Peter Mullen for several months. The nightmares that had vanished in the United States came back with a vengeance. My nights were punctuated with wild screams and my days with ferocious mood changes. One moment I would be laughing hysterically and the next in mournful tears. I could sense Bernie's bewilderment and helplessness.

Over the weeks I grew to love Bernie. She was a gentle soul who had never had children of her own and longed to mother someone. She and Peter wanted to adopt me and went as far as having legal papers drawn up. I rejected their offer with what must have appeared ingratitude and I know now that I hurt these two good people — but I was so afraid that if they knew about the real me they would want nothing to do with me. I was also fully aware that if they adopted me they would be landed with the further burden of contact with my grandmother and Basil and the rest of my troubled family, and that would have been as destructive in their lives as it had been in mine. Again I was protecting somebody other than myself. My rebuff must have come as a rude shock to Bernie and Peter. They could sense that I was not a normal teenager — but how could they be expected to know why?

As the weeks went by I developed an irrational fear that something terrible would happen to Bernie. The more I loved her the more fearful I became of her well-being. When she was in the house I never left her side. I stood close by her, shoulder to shoulder, determined to protect her at all costs. When she went to the toilet I stood outside the door waiting for her to come out. At night I would roll myself in a blanket and sleep just outside her door, determined that if Peter so much as touched her, I would spring upon him and wrench his eyeballs out of their sockets. Bernie became more and more threatened by my enervating love. In my desperation I drained her emotionally and spiritually, for she was too gentle to resist my need.

Finally the end came. I had settled down in Bernie's study to try to get through my homework. There had been little rain that year and Bernie's beloved garden was lying stunned and wilting under a breathless blanket. Even inside it was frantically hot and the heat stuck in corners, slid under doors, through cracks and finally into the study where I was trying to work.

Bernie came into the room and sat down silently beside me until I looked up at her. I wondered why her face was so sad.

"What's the matter, Bernie?"

She looked away. For a moment all I could hear was the chirpy tick-tock of the gold and glass clock on her desk. The stillness had an uncomfortable edge.

"Debs, these nightmares are getting too bad. The social worker and I feel that you need help in working through them. She ... there's a place ... Debs, I'm sorry, but you need to go away for a while to work things out."

"But I don't want to go away. I want to stay here with you and Peter."

"I know, I know. But we don't know what else to do for you, Debbie," she put her hand over mine, "there are people who can help you. Peter and I, well, we don't know what to do any more."

"How long will I have to be there?"

"I don't know. As long as it takes, I suppose."

"OK, I'll go if you say so. But you'll come and see me, won't you? You'll stay my friend?"

Bernie squeezed my hand. There were tears in her eyes. "Of course."

I believed her — and that made it all right to go. There wasn't much left to say. I knew that Maria Almeida, the social worker, had been to see Bernie and Peter and thought that they were just thoroughly weary of this odd child who had so abruptly refused their offer of adoption. Perhaps they truly didn't know how else to help me — and I couldn't bring myself to tell them the cause of all my suffering. More than anything I wanted Bernie and Peter to love and respect me. I desperately wanted to be their child, but if they knew what my father had done to me, if they knew about the men that Basil had arranged for me to service, and the photographs and all the other stuff, then I was absolutely certain they would not, could not, love me. I was unworthy of their love. Perhaps it was better if they put me away somewhere. It was the punishment I deserved. I tried to concentrate on my homework but the sums didn't make sense any more. The numbers were suddenly watery and dancing in front of my eyes. I went to the bathroom and furiously rubbed my face with a wet cloth. There was no point in finishing my homework. I wasn't going back to school anyway.

The next morning Bernie and I got into her car and drove north. In the wealthier northern suburbs of Johannesburg we drove past beautiful houses set in large park-like gardens. I didn't want to think about the place where I was going so I amused myself by imagining what it would be like to live in such homes, with servants and swimming pools and tennis courts. Then we went through some large iron gates decorated with big green harps. The name of the place was Tara.

Great palm trees shadowed the driveway and the gardens were filled with flowering shrubs. The main part of Tara, which was to become my home for the next four months, was a gracious old house with enormous stained glass windows in the hallway. Other more functional and ordinary single-storey buildings clustered round the feet of this main building like penitents round the feet of a venerable old saint. Later I discovered that this was once the home of one of the wealthiest families in Johannesburg. It was now converted into a place of safety and rehabilitation for people with mental problems.

Waiting at a side door was a nursing sister, her white uniform ramrod stiff. Bernie stopped the car close by her and I got out, dragging my suitcase, guitar and kangaroo after me. Bernie walked round the car, put her arms round me and gave me a swift hug.

"Aren't you coming in with me, Bernie?"

"No. I must go home now."

"Bernie, you promise you'll come and see me, won't you?"

Bernie looked away as she answered, "I promise." Then she got back into her car, waved at me and drove away.

I never saw Bernie again.

Chapter 11

"Everything's going to be all right, babe," the nurse said as I stood watching Bernie's car disappear down the driveway. She took my guitar and the stuffed kangaroo that Dell had given me and walked ahead of me up a narrow flight of stairs, her bum wiggle-waggling under the starched folds of her uniform. It didn't seem polite to watch her bottom so instead I counted the stairs, twenty in all, up to the small cement landing with its columns of bedraggled pot plants cheerfully surviving in rusty coffee tins. We walked to one of a row of doors.

"Come along, babe. I'll show you where you're going to sleep." She pushed open the door and we were in Ward 1. The room was large, airy and clean. But everything was grey: four grey hospital beds, four grey hospital lockers, grey curtains and grey floor tiles. The bed closest to the door was mine. On one of the other beds a young girl lay with her autumn hair spread on the pillow and her face to the wall.

Sister Andrews put my case down. "Geraldine, I've got company for you." After a few moments the girl turned her head and I could see that she had been crying.

"Now you get settled and I'll be back in a while." Sister Andrews bustled out, her black shoes squeaking on the polished floor.

There were bars on the windows, confirming my fear that my "badness" had finally landed me in jail. It took me a while to realise that this prison was to keep people out, not to keep me in. For the first time in my life I was truly safe. I was free from Granny May and most of all I was free from Basil. There was no one to watch out for. No one to hurt me. I lay back on the bed and closed my eyes. All I wanted to do was sleep.

The rationale behind sending me to Tara could be considered controversial. Never before had anyone as young as me been committed to Tara. I was going on fifteen at the time but I had a history of a suicide attempt, I was considered a habitual runaway by social workers who never once asked me what the problem was, and I had been taking large doses of tablets, tranquillisers and sleeping tablets, given to me by doctors at the South Rand and Johannesburg General Hospitals since the age of thirteen. I was suffering violent and seemingly inexplicable nightmares, mood swings and general confusion. The focus of the problem was always on my grandmother. Social workers did nothing to help me because my grandmother would always shift the attention onto herself and her problems: "But don't you see, I'm a pensioner and I have this child to contend with. I just can't manage," so social workers looked at what was happening in a very dysfunctional family rather than at the child who was affected by it. Not once did a social worker ask me if someone was hurting me and not once did I even hint at the true situation.

Having a granddaughter in a place like Tara was a great mortification to May and her constant complaint was "What will the neighbours think?" Jenny told me afterwards that May justified my being sent to Tara by saying "She's better off there, she's just like her mother." No wonder the social workers were very hard on her after I left — and perhaps under the circumstances the Social Welfare people just didn't have any alternative but to put me into Tara until there was place for me in a children's home.

At lunch time a bell woke me up and I walked down the stairs to a large dining room. There were long tables surrounded by bright blue plastic chairs. People were coming into the room in twos and threes. Some were talking but most were absorbed in their own silence.

A young man pulled out a chair for me. "Welcome to the loony bin. You look a bit young for this lot."

"I'm fifteen." Servants were moving about with plates of food.

"Hoo, boy. What have you been up to?"

I was silent. I had guarded my secret for so long that I no longer knew who or when to trust. "Who's that over there?" I pointed to a girl with arms like winter twigs. She was crying and trying to hide her pathetic face.

"That's Linda. She's anorexic. She won't eat. They have to force her. When they start, don't watch. It'll put you off your food."

Of course I watched. Two nurses marched across to the girl and hauled her upright. They kindly but firmly pushed her chair closer to the table and one held her down while the other tried to force the food into her mouth. Linda was crying and shaking her head. A thin howling stream of no-no-no came from her rounded mouth. Then she spat the food out. As the nurses pushed more food in, Linda gave a great heave and retched into her lap.

"There, I told you not to look. It's not nice but they have to do it."

"Why?"

"Why? Because she'll die if they don't."

Linda was allowed to leave the dining room and I watched her as she left. She was a fragile shadow, petal thin, her bones poking through her summer dress and her eyes sunk deep into her skull.

"She looks as if she's dead already."

"Yes, they all do."

I found out that most of the time we were allowed to do very much as we pleased. No activities were planned for the patients. There was a badminton court where we would play a few languid games, and once a week we were encouraged to go to group therapy. This was treated as a joke by the patients. Before we went in to the therapy room we would concoct weird stories for the therapists. We thought it was all a joke, but looking back now I see that if we had taken the situation seriously and used it for our own benefit we would all have been helped back to health by the dedicated and conscientious staff at Tara. I'm sure that the staff at Tara had their share of successes. I wasn't one of them.

After lunch on that first day I went back to Ward 1. Geraldine was still lying on her bed.

"Are we the only ones in this ward?"

She turned to me. "They come and go. It depends."

"Why are you here? If you don't want to talk about it ..."

"It's OK, really. I had a car accident a few months ago and I hurt my back. The doctors can't find anything wrong with it, but I'm always in such pain. They think I'm making it up. They think I'm mental or something when all the time I actually have something wrong with my back." She began to cry. "I can't make them understand."

I didn't know what to say. I just stood there watching the big, fat tears roll down her cheeks.

I had been in Tara for only a few days when Sister Andrews popped in to the ward. "Debbie, you have an appointment with Doctor Chatsworth in the morning. You go along and have a talk to him."

The psychiatrist's office was also grey, with a large government issue desk firmly in the centre of the floor. On the desk he had a notebook and a tape recorder. "All right, so you're Debbie. Yes, well, you'll be seeing me twice a week — Mondays and Thursdays — at this time. Try to be on time, will you."

I looked at the tape recorder. "Are you going to record everything I say?"

"Oh, yes," he said. "It's standard procedure."

That, I thought, was that. No way was I going to have my story on tape, to be used as evidence or blackmail or just for someone's perverted enjoyment. Somehow I was going to have to get through these twice weekly sessions and not give the game away. Besides, I didn't like him. He was a man and he was an authority figure. Double strike against him. Over the weeks I sat facing him, telling him the most awful garbage, stuff I presumed he wanted to hear, and all the time thinking to myself: "I wonder if I should try and seduce him. What would he do if I leant over the desk and felt him up? I could fuck this man any time I want."

Life in Tara fell into a dull miasma of routine. Each evening just before "lights out" everybody would form a long queue outside the night nurse's station. We were then issued with whatever drugs had been prescribed for us. It became a game. We would put the tablets under our dutiful tongues and walk away. Round the corner we would all spit our tablets out into a saucer. Then each person would take a couple of tablets and swallow them. The game was not to take our own prescription drug, it had to be someone else's. The idea was to see who got the best "buzz". I'm pretty sure that my record was unparalleled. One night I took two large pink capsules and after that I remember nothing until, two days later, I woke up in the ward strapped to my bed and on a drip. I had been found in a remote part of the garden in a cataleptic state. That was the last time any of us played tablet roulette.

No one bothered much about me after that. I could wander around Tara at will. The gardens were magnificent, with rolling lawns and flower beds filled with the colours of the rainbow. Unexpected tree-girdled nooks held secret benches where I could sit for hours just absorbing the loveliness and peace. For the first time in my life I became aware of the beauty and the healing potential of all natural things, from the large trees sweeping the sky with their soft branches down to the smallest frog and blade of grass. I would sit still, breathing in the quiet loveliness, drawing it down into the most injured places of my being, places so deep I could not, with my own will and power, bring succour to them.

I could walk unhindered down shadowed corridors where there were doors to other wards and I would pop in to "visit" whenever and whoever I chose. There was one door I tried to avoid, but its malevolent promise somehow drew me to it. Behind it was the shock treatment room and sometimes when I walked past there I could hear the patients screaming. Granny May had told me that my father had once undergone shock treatment, and had never been the same afterwards — but May was forever casting about for excuses for Basil, so who knows what the truth was. I would stand outside this door with a ghastly fear that it would fly open and my father be wheeled out.

One day my wanderings were interrupted by the sight of a woman being wheeled out to an ambulance. She was securely strapped to the gurney, her wild hair blowing over her face. When she saw me she called out, "They're taking me away. I'm going to a hotel in Sterkfontein. Come and visit me, won't you, dearie, and have tea."

I promised I would, but to return to Sterkfontein was unthinkable after those visits with Granny May. I added the thought of that woman being imprisoned there to my long list of night-time horrors and I would dream that it was me among the blank-eyed men and drooling babies, helpless and alone.

Maria Almeida came to see me and brought a load of school books but no one ever checked up to see whether I was studying or not. I was the only one doing any schoolwork — in fact, because I was the youngest person there, I earned the nickname The Tara Baby. It was only years later that an adolescent section was established.

Looking back, I realise that if it had been explained to me that I wasn't at Tara as a punishment but that a very sincere attempt was being made to help me sort out my confused life, perhaps I would not have been so guarded. Often I felt the truth well up like bile in my throat but each time I held back. Had I been made to feel that I was safe, who knows, maybe things would have been different. But abused children become the world's best actors and I rivalled the best that Hollywood had to offer. No one at Tara, or anywhere else, ever knew what had happened to me. They knew something was wrong but speculated that living with a ferociously domineering woman like May Reynolds could have triggered off my behaviour. And then I was twice rejected by my mother and no one could estimate what damage that could have done. I believed that in my silence I was doing a great job of protecting my family, that I was in control of my situation.

I saw Doctor Chatsworth twice a week for the four months I was there and not once did I reveal the truth. I wonder if he suspected that I was not being honest with him. If he did, he never said so.

The other patients at Tara were in much the same boat. If they were determined to get better then they cooperated with the staff. But many of them were not there of their own free will. Motivation had to be very strong to kick destructive habits and some of the patients were extremely sad cases.

Gustav was one for whom I felt a deep compassion. He washed his hands constantly, with soap and without soap, until the skin peeled off and hung in lacy sheets from his wrists. Linda was so severely anorexic that force feeding did little to help her. A few days after I was admitted she was taken to the Johannesburg General Hospital where she died not long after. There were drug addicts there and bulimics. There were men and women who had been emotionally battered by the stress of their everyday lives. There were people who had tried to commit suicide. So many in emotional and spiritual pain, I wished I could do something to help.

One of the advantages of being at Tara was that Granny May and Basil were forbidden to see me. My mother had tried to telephone from the States and had been told very politely that I wasn't taking any calls. Once or twice I phoned Bernie but when I heard the distance in her voice I put the phone down. I was unaware at the time of Bernie's sadness at being rejected by me. All I knew was that I had lost her. It was only years later that I realised that what I had interpreted as Bernie's rejection was in truth her terrible disappointment at not being able to help me. The only ones who came to see me were Jenny and Ruth. They never let me down. They were my constants, my link to a normal life, and seeing them once a week gave me a sense that I had not been totally abandoned.

It was at this time that Basil finally married the ever-faithful Tessa. It seems strange that, knowing what she knew about my father, Tessa still loved him enough to marry him. I often wonder whether she ever guessed what had been happening to me for so many years, but realise now that, even if she did, she was too weak to do anything to help herself, let alone me. And so often she was there to help, to take the beatings from Basil that were meant for me. And so the two misfits were married and between them lay the terrible knowledge of Basil's final act of rape. Jenny was embarrassed when she admitted to having gone to the wedding — and, at the time, that seemed a greater betrayal than the marriage. But, of course, Jenny never knew what my father was. She had left home before he started to abuse me and was mercifully spared both the deed and the knowledge of it.

At Tara the nightmares continued unabated. Most nights were peopled with men with soft skin and reaching hands that I could not evade. Through the night I would thrash and writhe and scream, trying to get away from their probing fingers and leering faces. Again and again I would throw myself off the bed and land heavily on the floor. Eventually the puzzled night nurses realised that it would be easier and safer if they just put my mattress on the floor. In time I managed to tame the worst of the nightmares by forcing them deep into my subconscious. This was a fatal mistake, as they were bound to resurface at another stress-filled time, which indeed they did. At least for the present I began to sleep at night.

The summer weather stayed warm and listless and then the leaves started falling. It felt as if I had been at Tara for a year. In early May when the trees were finally stripped bare by the cold autumn winds Maria Almeida came and told me that I was leaving. There was a place at a children's home in Johannesburg. I would stay there until I had finished my schooling and I didn't have to go back to Gran or to Basil.

I was about to start on the next part of my journey.

Chapter 12

At Epworth Children's Home I could be an ordinary child, doing children's things, being kid-naughty with the others. I did all the things that ordinary kids do, I bunked school, played tricks on the teachers and then got satisfyingly disciplined. Boundaries were set for me and I loved it. I was, however, deeply depressed. My few months in Tara had been the first time that I had space to think about what had gone before, and the more I contemplated my life the more saddened I became and the more fearful of my future. Now at Epworth the depression became full-flowered and disturbing. The school psychologist did her best to penetrate the wall of melancholy with which I surrounded myself but there wasn't much she could do, given my secretive nature. Trying to catch up on the school work I had missed also added to my anxiety. Emotional stress had dulled the instinct to learn. For so long there had been no space in my life for ambition other than that of survival. Now a fairly normal life required adjustments that I was ill prepared for.

I had not had any contact with my father from the time I left Vanderbijlpark, but I knew that he and Tessa were living somewhere in Germiston. Granny May came to see me and, for the first time, we were able to speak kindly to each other. Whether she was happy for me or for herself, I can't be sure.

"I'm so glad you're here, Debbie. Now I don't have to spend so much money on you," she said when I first went to Epworth, "I'm so glad that at last someone has realised that I've had enough."

May was then nearing seventy and I suppose she had every right to be relieved of the burden of what appeared to be a thoroughly rebellious teenager. I just wish that she had been able to see that there was someone else in the equation and that I had suffered too.

It was at Epworth that I had the first indications of what was to become my life's work. I found that I had an instinctive gift to counsel, to allow people to grieve or rage or just ventilate their inner emotions. More and more of the kids at Epworth would find their way to me when they were in trouble and I found that, by giving myself to them as a kind and sympathetic listener, I was slowly coming to the onset of my own healing. There were many girls in the home who had been through varying degrees of abuse and I could empathise with them and help them to an understanding of who they were and where they were going.*

Then one day the psychologist called me into her office. "I have some bad news for you, Debbie, your father passed away yesterday."

I sat looking at her.

"It's all right if you want to cry," she murmured sympathetically.

I didn't want to cry. I wanted to laugh and sing, I wanted to rejoice that at last I was free. But at the same time I felt a deep and anguished bitterness. He had died in his sleep, a peaceful passing which in no way expressed the brutality of his life. Why should a man who had inflicted so much hurt, so much humiliation, why should he be allowed to slip away quietly leaving me with the lifelong scars of his brutish treatment? I heard later that in his last months he had "repented" and turned to religion. This only made it worse for me. Why had he not been punished? I had hoped and expected that he would at least have suffered a painful and remorseful death. In my depression I began to doubt that there was indeed a loving God. If there was a God in the way I understood Him at that time, then my father should have been punished, not forgiven. There was also the deep regret — a feeling that will probably last until my own death — that I never had a real father and now it was too late.

At his funeral Granny May insisted that I go up to his coffin and kiss him goodbye. I did so to please her but felt crazy with rage at being forced to do something so obscene. What if he came back to life, rearing up from his satin-lined coffin to grab and hold me, I thought as I bent over his still form. I kissed him but hated myself and my grandmother for my hypocritical act.

Six weeks later Granny May came bustling into the Home. We were going shopping, she said. Jenny sat in the car, her face red and blotchy.

"What's up?"

"Tessa's dead. She blew her brains out. She's been lying in her flat for three

---

*We have found that 85% of the children who come to us have been abused in some way.
Headmaster, children's home, Gauteng.

days and nobody found her till today."

"Then why are we going shopping?" I protested.

"She doesn't have any more use for her credit cards so we might as well use them while we can." Granny May was cheerful as we drove to the dress shop. Rage seethed up from my solar plexus. Not at Granny May for her unfeeling greed, but strangely at Tessa, who had proved that she could not live without Basil. I wanted to shout to her — how dare you do this! How dare you blow your brains out after you had the courage to rescue me at two crucial points in my life, and then to go on living with my father, knowing what he was? How dare you, after my father gave you every kind of hell, not have the guts to live without him?

* * *

Then I met Wayne at a disco and fell in love. Granny May loved him too and began to push for us to get married. I wanted to please her. I wanted to please Wayne. It seemed the right thing to do. After all, I was complying with what society said was my rightful role in life, that of wife and mother. All round it seemed a good idea and I put aside my own doubts. I was seventeen and in my final year at school. When Wayne asked me to marry him I agreed.

The headmaster of the home was incredulous. "Debbie, you've six months to go before your Matric exam. I urge you to stay and see the year out. Surely there's no hurry?"

"I want to marry Wayne. I want to be happy," I said stubbornly.

"You will regret your decision. I can tell you now that I will be here having to look after your children one day."

"Over my dead body, sir."

At last I was going to be happy. At last something good was coming my way. Wayne was six years older than me and not only loved me as a sweetheart but ordered me around like a father. It was a perfect combination.

May was excited at the prospect of our marriage and urged that we marry right away. "You don't need to finish school. Wives don't need education. You won't have to go out and work, Debbie. Wayne will look after you and you'll be a wife and a mother."

May was married at seventeen and so was Jenny, so it was all right for me as well. The first few months were ecstatic. I was playing house. But soon the sheen of "housie-housie" began to wear thin and I asked Wayne if I could go and find a job.

"No way, my wife doesn't go out and work. My mother stayed at home and looked after her children, you must too."

Then I fell pregnant and my beautiful Bernadette was born. Her arrival papered over the cracks of our steadily deteriorating relationship for a while but finally our lives fell apart and in his frustration Wayne started to beat me. Suddenly the spectre of all the years of abuse came flooding in and I realised that if I stayed in this relationship it would start all over again. I had to leave. It was then that I found I was pregnant again.

After I'd packed my bags and found somewhere else to live I phoned Wayne. "I'm pregnant," I told him.

"It's not mine," he said.

"Oh, yes it is." But he refused to listen.

I was living in a damp, cramped caravan out of town with a baby that was constantly crying and cold. After one visit Wayne refused to allow Bernadette to come back to me. Maybe he was right, maybe I wasn't able to look after a baby, especially with another one on the way. At the end of my strength and courage, I allowed him and his mother to keep Bernadette. I had no choice.

It seemed that I was about to repeat the pattern set for me by my mother. In spite of my deepest promises to myself that I would never be like my parents and grandparents, here I was, abandoning my beloved child. And then I decided to have an abortion. I was sick with guilt, miserable at being alone after the early promise of happiness, and desperately lonely. I had begun to have a recurrent nightmare in which a mother, who could have been me or Myra, was abandoning a baby. The old pattern seemed to be asserting itself and I was terribly afraid that I would never be free from the past. Four months later Wayne's mother brought Bernadette back to me.

"I was the one who insisted that Wayne keep Bernadette, but I was mistaken," she confessed. "It was wrong of me to keep you apart."

I am sure that the failure of our marriage was due to my early conditioning. I married Wayne for all the wrong reasons: the need for security, enslavement to social mores, wanting to please my grandmother. In addition to that, I came into the marriage with too much baggage, nothing in the way of role modelling and no sound methods for dealing with the inevitable problems. I was fighting for my existence, my sense of individuality. Wayne wanted me to be someone I couldn't be. He became frustrated and eventually terribly angry and I bore the brunt of his helpless anger. I used the marriage as an attempt to escape the past and I was wrong. Because of my past we were doomed from the start. Two days after we were divorced Wayne remarried.

Then I met Mike. I was in bad financial, physical and emotional straits when Mike walked into my life. I was holding down two jobs in order to make ends meet and trying to care for Bernadette in between. Mike breathed life into what had up to then been only existence. There was no pretence with him. He was too real and he loved me totally and unconditionally. Wayne would withhold love if he was displeased with me but Mike loved me through it all. And as important, he loved Bernadette. We were married in November 1983.

With Mike I learnt that it was safe to be vulnerable. When we first met I was obsessed with control, and for Mike it wasn't easy. But as I gained a measure of peace with Mike I was able to let vulnerability seep in.

We had two children, Ryan and Robyn, and then we decided to move to Port Elizabeth, to make a new start.

It was there that I was to encounter the final and most obscene evil of my life.

Chapter 13

There was one more thread to unravel before we were free to leave Johannesburg. In the year before we left to start our new life in Port Elizabeth May Reynolds died. Some months before, there had been a phone call from the matron of the old age home where my grandmother lived. It was not the first time I'd had such a call. "Mrs Neville, you really have to find another home for your grandmother. We can't allow this kind of thing to happen again. It's too much, really. She's so aggressive and nasty to the other old ladies and, quite frankly, we've had enough."

"This kind of thing" was Granny May getting into fights with other old ladies and doing them quite a lot of physical damage. Old age had done nothing to mellow her. This time she had shaken another old lady around by her hair, and actually pulled a clump out. As a child her behaviour had been an unending source of shame for me, and even though it was obvious that May was the instigator of her own misery, the child in me always felt "guilty". This was one of the reasons why I spent so much of my life try-ing, in my own childish way, to "protect" her from hurt.

Then came an incident which, I believe, led to my grandmother's death. There was to be a concert at the home and May was asked to sing. She was tremendously excited by the project and saw it as the start of a new phase in her singing career. Pat Loubser, her accompanist from the old days, was going to play for her and she would sing some of her old favourites. May chose her best dress and a pair of sparkling diamanté earrings and subdued the growing butterfly flutters in her stomach with a stiff brandy. I had been invited to the concert and sat with bated breath as Granny May walked proudly onto the small stage. Pat played the opening bars of the first song. May stood there and no voice came. Pat started again but again May's voice was gossamer and snow flakes. She walked off the stage a broken woman and not long after that she was dead.

Even in death I was controlled by Granny May's wishes. I sat by her as she lay dying in the hospital. Towards the end she grabbed my hand and held on with surprising strength. "Debbie, when I'm gone there's some things you must do for me. You must put my teeth in and you must cut my toenails. I can't go without my teeth in and my toenails cut. Promise me you'll do that."

"I promise, Gran."

When her hand slacked in mine there were no stirrings of grief. All I could think of was that I still had to obey her and carry out her last demands. The night sister held my shaking hand as I slipped her teeth into her slack mouth, but I couldn't bring myself to cut her toenails. My mind was screaming *it doesn't matter any more*, but even at this moment I was still emotionally bound by the years of control over my life.

We left Johannesburg with a sense of relief. Now we could really live a more gentle, stress-free life. Mike deserved this. However understanding he had been in the past, I was glad that, at last, he would be free of my family's unending problems.

We hadn't been long in Port Elizabeth when my mother phoned me from California to wish me a happy birthday. It was the first time that she had spoken to me since my abortive stay with her so many years before. I was sure of the reason. "She's going to die, Mike. That's why she phoned."

Not long after, I got a phone call from Jane, my step-sister, to tell me that Myra was dying. As I put the phone down I was overwhelmed by the need to go to my mother and "make things right" for her. I contacted the hospital in the States and they confirmed what Jane had told me, that my mother was near death. Her alcohol habit had finally caught up with her.

Once again my overriding sense of duty kicked in. I had to talk to her before she died. Mike was patient and understanding.

"Debs, if that's what you have to do, then go."

Dell met me at the airport. "Honey, she's waiting for you. She knew you would come."

"But how did she know?"

"Search me," Dell shook his head, "she's in a coma and she's just waiting for you before she'll let go."

He took me to the hospital and watched my face as I looked at this pathetic little bundle that was my once beautiful mother. I held her hand and it was like holding a bunch of dry stalks. "Mom, I'm here. It's me, Debbie." I felt a small tightening of her hand and thirty minutes later Myra died, her hand still in mine.

We walked slowly out into the night air. Dell put his arm around me. "It's crazy, honey. She never stopped talking about you, telling everyone about her wonderful daughter. She idolised you, put you on a pedestal. I still don't understand why she treated you so badly when she had the chance to make things right for you."

"It's over, Dell."

"Yes, thank God it's over, for all our sakes."

Dell took me home and there in the living room were many of the friends who had welcomed me when I was thirteen and had been silent witnesses to Myra's second rejection of me. They told me of Myra's remorse at having abandoned her three girls and her great love for me. "Every time we went to the store and Myra saw little girl's dresses, she'd break down and cry and I'd have to take her home," one told me.

"Yes, and then she would drink herself into oblivion, because she couldn't face the pain," said another.

Someone else told me how Myra always believed that I would come back to the States and "make everything right for her". "Phone Debbie, she'll come over and make it right," she would say when her life became unbearable.

It was evident from what her friends had to say that Myra never forgave Granny May for driving her away from her children. I sadly recognised that she too found it easier to blame someone else for the tragedies in her life and could not bear to face her own role in what had happened. At her funeral a Navy chaplain said, "Myra was one of the best loved people in our community. Although she drank so heavily she still managed to live her life with compassion for those in need." Except for me in my need, I grieved. Strange that when she had the opportunity of making up for what she had done to me, she found it impossible.

And so another of those whose influence had brought me to adulthood was dead. The three people who forged my life and made it what it was were gone. Basil, Myra and May, each of them part of a destructive trio, each in their own way responsible for the loss of my childhood. At last I was free, or so I thought. But I still had a long journey ahead and many lessons to learn.

In Port Elizabeth I joined Childline and found, as in Epworth, that I was a natural-born counsellor. Working with children, helping them find themselves, was a particular joy. I felt that I knew what was going on in their lives. After all, I had been there too. I could feel for them, I could solve their problems, I could get in there and "make it right" for them. In most of the cases I worked on I believe I was able to make a significant difference, not realising that the motive behind it all was so terribly unbalanced. What it did was to keep me in control. If I could influence another child's life then I wouldn't have to look at my own. It was easier to look at another child's pain than confront my own. I could not, dared not, look at the child within me, but there was an emptiness within that signalled my deep longing to "make things right" for myself. Joining Childline meant that it was safer to look at abuse through the eyes of another child. It was distanced and I could cope with it.

Childline was good for me and I was good for Childline. It was as a result of my work there that one of the hospitals contacted me and asked me to take over their créche. Like all other jobs I tackled this one with great energy and enthusiasm. It wasn't long before I had 140 kids and ten staff members. Kids that came to us unhappy and troubled seemed to thrive. Some of the teachers began to feel threatened because I was like a modern-day Pied Piper, gathering all the children to me and loving each one of them with an unusual passion. Again, I was pouring into these children all the love that I couldn't give to my own inner child. I could control the love I gave to them, so it was safer for me. I found out later that this is a typical symptom of an abuse survivor. We have to be in control, we tackle things that would daunt other people and most often we succeed. We have to succeed to prove our self-worth. We are always looking for approval, trying to please others, trying to make the world right. We are always looking for and getting praise and then feeling that we have to do more and more in order to maintain the level of esteem.

The créche was a demanding job but one in which I found great satisfaction. I did a good job but the cost to myself and my family was enormous. In the process of trying to win the approval of everybody I often forgot my own family. I found that I could love other people's kids in a way that I couldn't always love my own. Perhaps they were too near to me and I was too vulnerable to their love to feel safe loving them in the way that I would have liked. Fortunately, Bernadette, Ryan and Robyn were happy, well-adjusted children whose self-confidence allowed me to spread my wings and experience realities other than those of housewife and mother. Life generally was pretty good. Mike and I were deeply involved in our church and ran the various youth groups. Bernadette, Ryan and Robyn were happy in school and life had become worth living.

The last Christmas we were to have in Port Elizabeth, we were asked to foster three children, Isabella, aged eleven, her sister Sharon, aged five, and Jason, aged three. Welfare had rescued them from an abusive family situation and needed temporary foster parents just over Christmas. Mike and I were happy to take them in. For me the word "abuse" was a trigger word and I would have done anything for them, while in Mike's loving heart there is always room for more.

Three year old Jason had been physically and emotionally starved and he would sit on the floor shovelling food into his mouth, his eyes darting everywhere, terrified that he wouldn't get more. He didn't know how to sit at the table and eat with a fork or a spoon. He trembled constantly, had a severe stutter and was dirty and emaciated when he arrived at our house. Five year old Sharon didn't know how to use a toilet; she would go to the dustbin in the corner of our bedroom and hunch over it. We had to teach her how to use the toilet and how to flush afterwards. We also taught her and the other two how to bathe in the great white bathroom next to their bedroom. They didn't even know how to keep themselves clean. As a family I believe that Bernadette, Ryan and Robyn, even though they were only thirteen, seven and five at the time, did most of the healing work there. All they did was to accept the failures and pathetic weaknesses of the three newcomers and love them unconditionally. It was a strange Christmas having three kids so badly traumatised by their parents. Our unconditional love for them created a secure space where they could begin to heal from the traumas of parental abuse and we learned how to deal with such trauma. For example we learned to feed Jason small bits and pieces through the day so that he was never hungry enough to panic about his next meal. He learned to eat with a fork and spoon and Sharon soon became toilet trained. By the time they left to go to a more permanent foster home they were relatively calm and sociable.

It taught me that if you just love children and treat them with respect and fairness, then all things are possible. It was an important lesson for me, because I learned just how important it is to love a child so that they can grow strong and straight and true, like a silver birch tree. The negative side was twofold. I felt strongly the deprivation of my own childhood and was all the more determined to do everything I could, heal any wound, make any child happy. But my motives were all wrong. I was doing it for myself, and not for them.

The greatest stumbling block to my success, although I didn't recognise it at the time, was my need to control. From control came the inevitable manipulation. Without realising it, I was using the same techniques that my grandmother used, albeit more tenderly than she managed. Control and manipulation, a recipe for disaster.

But my years with Childline were good years and I learned much about myself and about others. Now I was ready, I thought, to tackle more. Now I was ready to "make it right" for the world.

Chapter 14

In November 1992 Mike was offered a job back in Johannesburg and he left Port Elizabeth to start with his new employers while the children and I waited for the end of the school term.

One evening after supper I went to visit a friend in hospital. It was a dark night and as I parked the car a face appeared at the driver's window. As I turned to talk to the man another one slid into the passenger seat and held a knife to my throat.

"I don't have anything," I whispered. "Take the car. It doesn't matter."

"It's not the car we want, pretty little lady. It's you. We want to have some fun."

As the other man slipped into the back seat of the car I thought back to the time in my childhood when I could use a switch-off mechanism. It's just going to be sex, I thought, you can handle this, you have before. All you have to do is slip away like you used to. Remember how to do it, Debbie, you don't have to be here.

I don't remember where they told me to drive — all the while they were feeling me, touching me, kissing me, holding the knife to my throat. Then on a dark stretch of veld they told me to stop and they dragged me out. In the scuffle my shoes came off, and I kept wondering *where are my shoes, I mustn't lose my shoes, they're new, Mike's going to be mad if I lose my shoes.* They dragged me over some sandy earth close to the beach and into the bushes, then they tore off my panties and then my blouse and bra. Then they threw me down. They were laughing.

Debbie, just switch off, I thought. Use all the old techniques, you can do it. It'll soon be over.

But I couldn't. I couldn't go back. I couldn't retrieve that nothingness into which I had escaped as a child. I was there with everything they did to me. I knew it all and felt it all.

Just stay alive, Debbie. The kids need you.

Stay alive, Mike loves you.

Just stay alive.

I tried at one stage to fight but they picked up rocks and beat my head until the blood ran down from my face and was sucked up by the dry beach sand. When they stabbed me in the stomach I lay stunned and quiescent. But these men were determined to abuse me to the utmost. They violated me in ways that even the paedophiles of Durban could not have imagined. They forced me to fellate them and then they urinated on me. They took turns at raping me and then they raped me together, one raping me and the other sodomising me. Mercifully I blanked out, for the pain was unbearable.

When I came to they were gone. I was bleeding heavily from the wound in my stomach. My hands and arms were cut where I had tried to defend myself. There was blood and semen and urine everywhere. Strangely, they had left my car. My clothes were torn in pieces but I wrapped the shreds around me and drove away. I don't remember much about the rest. I got to the police station and I remember one small young policewoman, her face white and stricken, saying over and over, "I'm so sorry. I don't know what to say, I don't know what to say." I screamed at her, "Then just shut up", some of my immense anger seeping through the shock and the pain.

The District Surgeon was called but I was told that he couldn't come to me, I would have to get to his offices at the hospital as best I could. I was half naked but forced to walk, dirty, tangled and bleeding, through the hospital where I worked. I felt the humiliation of being seen by friends and colleagues who stood dumb and irresolute, until two of them ran for a blanket and a wheelchair.

The District Surgeon was rough and silent. I wish he had told me what he was doing. It would have been easier to bear the further prying and poking I had to endure. The irony of it! A few months earlier, I had joined Life Line and become a rape counsellor. I was the one who told rape victims to report their rape, to go to the District Surgeon, lay a charge, do everything by the book. And now, when it happened to me, I was devastated by the lack of care and concern being shown to me. They were so busy with their paper work, the surgeon and the police, that they didn't, perhaps couldn't, allow themselves to see a violated human being. I was only a number. Not once did the District Surgeon look at my face, look into my eyes. Perhaps he was afraid: he might have seen his own daughter or wife lying there.

At last I was allowed to go home. All I wanted was to get into the shower before the children saw me, but I was too slow. Bernadette was awake and saw me, my face swollen, both eyes bruised and purple, my lips split and my cheeks scraped, my body a mass of welts and wounds, and above all, the smell. She began screaming and I pulled her into the shower with me. I turned the water on and we stood hugging each other and crying.

"Just let me tell you what happened. I'm going to be all right, just let me tell you."

The next morning the newspaper headlines screamed — "Local woman gives hitch hikers lift — gets raped". I went berserk and grabbed the phone.

"How dare you. I was raped, then the police and the district surgeon violate me again and now the media. How dare you do this to me. Why don't you just put there: 'Woman gets raped by the media' — it would be nearer the truth." The editor was calm, dispassionate and disinterested. "Then why not tell us the real story," he said.

"Why didn't you get the story right the first time instead of blackening my name? Isn't it enough that I've been raped and stabbed, but you have to make it worse for me and my family by making me out to be a fool and a liar?" By evening the newspaper had retracted the story and set things right; that the woman in question had not picked up hitch hikers but had been kidnapped out of a parking lot. But, as far as I was concerned, the damage was done.

The next day the police asked me to take them to the place where the rape had taken place. I was a blank, I couldn't remember where it had happened. We drove around for what seemed like hours until I recognised the spot and the cops began their work. I stood next to the police car for about three hours while they fossicked in the bushes, bringing me various pairs of women's panties, always asking, "Are these yours?" It seemed that this was a favoured spot for these two evil young men, for there were about five pairs of panties, not counting mine. Back at the police station the police told me to wait while they had their lunch, and I sat in the charge office for over an hour until they were ready to take me back home.

Something happened to me in that hour. I must have decided that the way I had been treated by the two men, by the authorities and by the media had made it too difficult to go on living. I stopped eating, drinking, sleeping. I stopped functioning. I sat, never moving, my eyes glazed and unseeing. People were in and out of my life; who they were, I don't know. Mike came home but it didn't seem to matter. The children touched me with gentle hands, trying to call me back from the far-off place to which I had moved, but I didn't feel them. I wanted to die.

Eventually I was hospitalised and treated for dehydration and malnutrition. While I was there the police arrested the two men and then released them, as they told Michael, because they claimed I had paid them to do it.

My peaceful, mild, beloved husband blew. "What! You saw her, you fools! Do you think anybody would pay for that? Are you mad?"

The policeman shrugged. "Now, don't get upset."

I was heavily tranquillised with Prozac or Valium or whatever, but my reaction to the drugs was to become more suicidal than ever and one night the staff of the hospital found me on a window ledge high above the street.

I don't remember much — and yet I remember too much. All the peace of mind that I had fought so hard to gain, was gone. The control I had used to reconstruct my life and hold my psyche together was smashed away. I had nothing, no protection, my soul was naked. The nightmares which had tormented my childhood returned. This time, not only my father and the paedophiles but now the two rapists were also present. Once again my mattress was placed on the floor by the concerned hospital staff.*

Just before the kids and I were due to leave Port Elizabeth we got a call from the police. They had lost my file. All the evidence from the District Surgeon, my statement, everything.

I went to the police station and withdrew the charges. One cop sat laughing at me but another begged me to reconsider, "Please don't do this, lady, we have to nail them, otherwise they'll just do it again to some other young woman." But I couldn't. The guilt of the past and the destruction of my childhood had burst through like a volcano. I had had no rights as a child and no one had protected me; now, as an adult, I still had no rights and still had no one who could or would protect me. Was there any justice in the world for women and children?

"Where are you, God?" I screamed. "Why? Why so much? How much more do I have to go through? This is enough. I can't. Please, I beg you. Dear God, no more!" And this time God listened.

It was to be the end of the physical abuse in my life but it was not yet over and my fragile craft had yet some way to go before entering a safe harbour.

---

*In 1995 two men were convicted of the attempted murder and rape of "Allison". The media called them the "Satanist rapists". These were the two men who raped me.

Chapter 15

My withdrawal of the case against the two rapists had a very bad effect on me. Suddenly I was sucked back into the childhood trauma that I had fought so hard to ignore. One of several incidents in my childhood now stood out starkly. When I was thirteen we had a family gathering in Granny May's flat. There was Jenny and her husband, Basil and Tessa, Granny May and myself. I made tea for everybody with an ill grace and brought the tea tray in to the lounge. I saw my grandmother whisper something to Jenny. Jenny shook her head and then shrugged. As I put the tray down Jenny and Basil tackled me and pulled me down onto the carpet. Then Jenny jerked my panties off. Everybody started laughing at me as I tried to cover my nakedness. Granny May laughed so much at my red face and burning ears that the tears poured down her fat cheeks. Then on that summer night in Port Elizabeth two men did the same thing to me — and all the humiliation, all the loss of dignity, the remembered inability to protect myself, all came forth in a flood.

My adult life had been sustained by the control I had over every situation and every emotion. Now I had been overtaken by events over which, like my childhood, I had no control. It was as if a great door which had closeted my emotions had now swung wide and everything burst out in a great heave of anger, humiliation and shame. With the rape I experienced everything I had felt as a child all at once, all piled on top of one another, threatening to smother any new life I might have hoped for. In going to Port Elizabeth I hadn't run away from anything, I had run to the excavation of my past.

The system that had not helped me as a child, had not protected me, had let me down again as an adult. As a child one tends to believe that things are going to be better when one grows up; I now learned the hard way that this wasn't necessarily so. In the past I had survived because I had been able to keep the Debbie-child and the Debbie-adult apart. Then two men walked into my life and it was no longer possible to separate the child from the grown-up Debbie. Now I was being forced to face the child within.

We left Port Elizabeth as soon as I was strong enough to drive to the Transvaal. Mike had found a pleasant house in Krugersdorp and we settled down to what was outwardly a normal life. I needed to work and the thing I did best was counselling so I took a job at a place called The House in Hillbrow. The House was a refuge for prostitutes and drug addicts in Johannesburg's then notoriously dark underbelly. Soon I found myself counselling the prostitutes and pouring all my energy and emotions into a job that by its nature could have precipitated even a well-balanced person into severe depression. Perhaps it was to be expected that my body would rebel against the punishment I was inflicting on myself and I began to have black-outs. When this happened I wouldn't know where I was, where I had been or how I got there. One night I rear-ended another car. I had blacked out behind the wheel. I began to experience severe panic attacks, any-where, in the supermarket, in the car, at home, in The House. I began to feel that, suddenly, I was no longer safe, that my facade was crumbling, that my blockades had been breached and I was about to come face to face with God alone knew what? The ghosts of my past? Myself?

One evening Mike walked into the bedroom to find me sitting up in bed holding a razor blade, the blood pumping from my arms onto the walls and blankets.

Before the rape I lived and I breathed but I didn't feel. The control I had over my life and my emotions was the generator that kept my life in motion. But I felt nothing; no emotion, no hate, no anger, no passion, nothing. I told Mike bits of my story, and it was easy to tell because it was someone else's story, not mine. I was the adult and the story was about some kid, a pathetic little wimp who was never allowed to question the adults in her life but just had to obey, one who couldn't even look after her-self. The adult Debbie wasn't like that. I was in control of every situation. I could manipulate every situation. I never needed anybody. I was a strong, capable person. If anything I felt a contempt for that child because she had been too weak and frightened to stop the abuse. Indeed, I was angry with her because she never stopped loving her father and her granny. In spite of all they did to her, in spite of knowing that what they did to her was unjust, she still loved them.

As a child I had longed for the love of at least one of the adults in my life and because of all that happened my nurturing needs were unnaturally linked with sex, however painful and unpleasant, and I had not learned how to meet my need for unconditional love in a healthier way. Now the adult dared not look into the eyes of that child in case she saw herself.

The only certainty I had in life was that I needed to break the pattern. I had to prove to May, to Basil and Myra, even though they were dead, and to myself that I could make it, that I was all right, that I was going to be better than they had been. In that desperate desire to be as unlike them as possible were the seeds of a different destruction. There were certain emotions like anger and outrage that I couldn't allow myself to feel because Basil and May and Myra had felt them and they had used them destructively, one by raping and abusing me, one by destroying my self-esteem and one by abandoning me not once but twice. I never allowed myself to get angry. As a child I had no suitable example, I had not seen anyone using emotions constructively so, as an adult, I had no legitimate outlet for all the pent-up rage and hatred. People noticed what a calm, controlled person I was — but deep down, it wasn't like that at all. Even Mike saw me as a competent and capable person, so when I eventually collapsed it must have been very hard for him. Once again the nightmares returned and in the mornings he would ask about what I had said in my plagued sleep, and these were the only opportunities we had of exploring my past together. Even then I was unable to share much of what had happened.

But now the rape was with me every day. I punished myself because I couldn't control what had happened. I couldn't blot out what they had done to me as I had when my father, his friends or the paedophiles had abused me. I felt labelled by a critical society, the police, the District Surgeon, the media, all of which had in one way or another conspired to make me feel that I was to blame for what had happened. In my childhood I never told anyone what was happening to me because I was so sure they wouldn't believe me. Then as an adult when I was raped I thought that if I told people they *would* believe me — and they didn't. When I had the courage to look back I felt justified in not having told anyone about the childhood abuse. "Society" had proved that it couldn't be trusted. I couldn't prevent the abuse as a child and I couldn't prevent the rape. That was the bottom line, but I felt guilty on more than one count. Most rape victims do feel a sense of guilt, but for me there was a double dose. There was the child within and the adult without suddenly finding commonality in a dreadful experience. I wasn't ready to accept that the two Debbies were part of the whole. I wasn't ready for these great surges of emotion that stormed my citadel and my defences. I had been unfeeling for too long, now I was being forced to feel again.

That night in a fever of fear Mike rushed me to hospital, my arms and body cut and bleeding. I can honestly say now that it wasn't a suicide attempt. There was just so much anger in me, anger at my family, at society, and above all anger at myself, that I had to let it all out — and I didn't know any constructive way to deal with that anger. The only way I knew was the way my family had known, by breaking things and hurting other people.*

---

*If the adults around you were out of control with their feelings, you got the message that feelings led to violence or destruction. Anger meant beatings or furniture thrown across the room.

The courage to heal, by Ellen Bass and Laura Davis, p. 35.

The casualty staff at the local hospital stitched me up, sedated me and left me to sleep. A week later I was sent to recuperate at a small nursing home for mental patients. I remember sitting there for hours, looking out of the window at the trees and the sky, feeling how good it was to be mad like everybody else in the home. I wanted to be mad, to let go of the responsibility of hanging onto sanity. Here in the nursing home I could be what I wanted and it was OK. I was teetering on the edge of insanity. There was nothing inside any longer, no desire to fight or control or to love or even to exist. It was almost as if my soul had vacated my body. I could have slipped over into the abyss and not come back. It was a comfortable feeling, allowing my mind to slip away. No more having to feel. No more commitment or responsibility. No more physical body to be hurt.

But somewhere in the drugged recesses of my mind I knew that if I gave up then Gran and Basil and Myra would have won. I wasn't sure of how much more I could stand, how much more was going to be expected of me, how much more I would have to do to become a normal human being, but I knew deep down that life wasn't finished with me yet and I had to go on.

I wonder now what it was that helped me turn the corner. Perhaps it was all the prayers that were being said for me by so many people, perhaps it was the one good family trait instilled in me by Granny May — never give up. I only know that one day I got dressed and asked to be allowed to go home.

By this stage both Mike and I realised that I needed help in sorting out my past and I reluctantly started therapy with Emma, a psychotherapist in Weltevreden Park. I realise now that it was important to have someone like Emma in my life. It is almost impossible to heal from childhood sexual abuse in isolation. The damage that is done to a child is compounded by the air of secrecy and silence in which the abuse takes place and keeping silent only perpetuates the abuse into adulthood.

It was hard, but with Emma's help I began to unfold my past. The pain was so deep that there were times when I doubted that Emma and I would ever reach and heal it, but she had a way of gently probing until she reached a point where I would back away. She challenged me but I was scared, and harsh on myself. With Emma I found myself in a place where someone in authority, someone I could trust, was saying *what your father did was wrong*. At first I couldn't accept that. I made excuses for him; yes, but, it was Gran. Yes, but, he was drinking. Yes, but, shame, poor Dad, he didn't have a chance. Shame, poor Gran, what she had to put up with. Yes, but, poor Mom. With Emma I had to work through all that, finally to acknowledge that, indeed, what they did to me was wrong. There were no excuses to be made, no rationalisation, no justification. I was conditioned to think up all the excuses in the world as to why they did what they did. Now here was Emma telling me that it wasn't like that at all. That abusing a child is wrong, full stop.

"Get angry, you have a right to," she said. But I couldn't, because somewhere inside was a child's voice saying that if I got angry Emma wouldn't care about me any more and I would adversely affect the one relationship I needed in order to heal.

"Why be angry at people who are all dead? What's the point?"

Emma would gently remind me, "But, Debbie, you're not dead, and it is your right to be angry with them for what they did to you. You have a right to feel what is essentially a normal human response to injustice."

In doing this inner-child work I became aware of what it meant to feel. I had so much compassion and feeling for others and yet none for myself. Perhaps it was too dangerous to feel for the inner child, so I poured all my love and empathy into others. Before the rape I hadn't faced the important issues in my life. With Emma I had to look at my childhood — and instead of telling a story about someone else, I had to feel my way through my own story with emotions unused to the thorny and painful path.

We battled, Emma and I, to get to a point where I could feel for that inner child. There were many times when I walked out of Emma's office angry with her, angry with myself. Even that was a triumph, because I was feeling, even if it was only anger.

"Look at it, Debbie."

"Why? For what?" I back-pedalled every time she challenged me to look at the child I had been.

"You have to nurture that child, Debbie."

"No! Not nurture. Nurture is softness and soft lips and hairless chests. I can't tolerate 'nurture'. Don't use that word."

I didn't recognise the word as meaning feeding, cherishing or sustaining. For me the word "nurture" triggered off a series of emotions that forced me to examine the things I had done, the way I would go looking for sex, in order to draw to me the "love" or the "nurturing" that I needed. I will always carry a certain amount of guilt about that, although I understand, rationally, that I knew no other way. There were times throughout my life when I felt the need to have control over men, any man. I had misplaced my anger and bitterness at not being able to control my father and quenched it with my need to conquer and manipulate the other men who came close to me. At times in therapy I would feel the need to go out and see if I could still do it.

In Emma's office I would weep bitterly, terrified that I was slipping back into past patterns. Those were the times when I could smell my father, feel his presence in her rooms. My throat would close up and I would feel suffocated by my impotence to save myself from him. Then I would run from her office in cold panic.

The next week Emma would be there for me again. I had to go back and learn how to feel. It was tough; I wanted Emma to do the feeling for me. Instead she firmly guided me to realising that I had to do it for myself.

This book has gone a long way to unearthing what happened and why. There will always be parts that I haven't exposed as they wouldn't serve any purpose. It has been difficult to verbalise the extent of what happened to me because there are no words to describe the abasement and the degradation and the terror of my young life. When I read what my friend Jenny had written I sometimes thought, "But, it wasn't like that at all. It was worse," and yet I can't describe how much worse it was, and so these words on bald white pages will have to suffice. Only that little girl who suffered so much would be able to tell the whole story — and sometimes it is still hard to find her.

Therapy helped me to connect with the inner child. I learned to look for her and see her and, eventually, cry for her. She wasn't the pitiful puppet that I had believed she was, instead I found that she was a helpless, frightened little girl. I had been very hard on her and when I started feeling for her the tears came. Poor little girl. Poor, poor little one, so lost and afraid. At last someone is loving you.

In Emma's office I remembered something that took place when I was still very young. There was a grassy lane between two houses not far from us. Most of the year the grass was tall enough to hide me and I would often creep between the waving stalks and sit in a corner and dream. My dreams were of a Daddy who could love me and not hurt me, and a Mommy who would put her arms round me and protect me. I dreamed of how I would like people to see me, the real me, and how they would love me. I promised myself that when I grew up I was going to be the kind of person that everybody could love, like Ruth. And when I grew up that was what I tried to do. But it was only in Emma's office that I learned about the complexities of love. I began to understand that I had to love and forgive the little girl Debbie before I could love the adult she had become. I learned that I couldn't expect anyone else to love me unless I loved myself first — and I also learned that I had to love myself first before I could begin to love others.

Basil and Granny May and my mother were effective teachers in that they taught me the negative side of anger, the negative side of happiness. No good things; no joy, no humour, no passion. If you were angry then you were violent. If you didn't smash things then it wasn't anger. You had to be ugly to people, that was how it was. You spoke ill of everybody, you swore at people, you pulled their hair out — or you let people beat you and trample all over you.

When I grew up I decided that I had to turn that all around and be exactly the opposite to what they had been, what they had taught me. I was an ultra-nice, ever-capable person; there had to be no fault in me. I hadn't realised that ugliness and beauty, pain and joy, love and fear, are so inextricably joined that there can't be one without the other, and that in realising and accepting this paradox, the duality of human experience, we become enriched.

When those two men came into my life they broke the shell in which I had enclosed my feelings and emotions. Even in that terrible event, I can see now, there was the seed of good. I became a feeling person. Patiently Emma allowed me the space to build up my courage and in my own time explore those dank marshes where my personal rank weeds grew. It was in her office that I learned to feel, to become strong enough to be vulnerable, to be tough enough to be gentle, to be in control only enough to keep chaos at bay, for in that is life truly and satisfyingly lived.

I now see the breakdown which started when I slashed myself with the razor blade as a good thing. Afterwards I began to have a quality of life that had not been there before. I began to see things in colour. Before, my vision was only black and grey and white. Until very recently my home was only a roof and four walls where we could shelter and eat and sleep. Now I'm starting to allow myself to like things, to want pretty things, flowers in vases and nice pictures on the walls, and clothes that are blue or green. I can now hear birdsong and have learned that roses and mint and fresh sheets smell good.*

I was always there for everybody else. Now at last I have given myself permission to be there for myself. I have grown used to the concept that I am worthy of self-esteem. I am beginning to like myself a lot.

This book has probably been the final step in my healing process, although it would never have come about if I not had the breakdown. I would have continued to limp along until some other crisis precipitated me headlong into a final step to recovery. I will always have the scars of sexual abuse and rape. I am handicapped and I must learn to live with that, not only live but thrive. It is possible. I am finding the way and nowadays it has become an exciting and worthwhile journey.

I sometimes wish that Basil, May and Myra were all still living. I would like to ask my father one question — why, why did you do that to me? But more than that one question I wish they could see that, whatever they did to me, I am here, I have survived, and my life has beauty and purpose and worth.

---

*Eventually you get to where life is technicolor, and it's worth it.

The courage to heal, by Ellen Bass and Laura Davis, p. 64.

Chapter 16

Looking back, I see that the streets of Hillbrow seemed a good place to sublimate my mental and emotional conflict after the rape. The streets were mean and dirty. The pavements smelled of urine and rotten fruit. On every corner a few overpainted girls would stand. The prostitutes have moved out now. Hillbrow has become too ugly even for them, but when I worked there at The House as a counsellor and friend there was still some semblance of order in the busy cosmopolitan streets.

I saw a lot of me in the girls who nightly paraded the streets or worked in the clubs. Over and over I realised it could have been me, had my life not taken the turns it had. I could so easily have slipped into the realms of that particular Hades that I felt a special rapport with the girls who had.

I found the prostitutes living in extremely squalid conditions in seedy clubs, hotels or bedsitters in Hillbrow. Often they would phone me up and say, "Debbie, please help me, I've just OD'ed," and I would go to them wherever they were, where the air was fetid with cheap perfume and the familiar musty smell of dagga.

I grew to love the girls and when they recognised that my love was unconditional they trusted me. We would spend hours together, sometimes sitting on the street corners drinking coffee out of polystyrene cups, just talking. They would tell me of their dreams of having a nice home and children and a kind husband who came home at night. Often they would tell me about the "steamers" they had the night before, how they'd been physically hurt and how they reacted to some particularly uncouth man. It was OK to tell me. They felt safe with me. I learned about the Hillbrow culture, their religion, their shifting sexual relationships with other girls and with their pimps. Often they would tell me about their other, earlier, lives when they were children at home, and what had driven them onto the streets. It was terrible to hear about the damage parents often inflicted on their children. I discovered that most of the girls on the streets had been abused by a male authority figure when they were small. I suppose that's why I related so well to them. I understood what it was like to live in a severely dysfunctional and abusive family. I became an inspiration to them as they realised that they didn't have to give in to their circumstances. If I could survive, then they could.

Astrid was one of my favourite girls. She had a corny sense of humour and very rarely let things get her down. Astrid had led a fairly normal life until her three year old daughter died of meningitis. In their grief her family turned on her and blamed her for the little girl's passing. Astrid could not cope with her grief and the guilt that was piled on her by her family and it drove her onto the streets of Hillbrow. She became a drug addict and a prostitute. The death of her child could not have been the sole factor in her downfall but she could not bring herself to tell me more.

One morning I sat with her at The House and she told me that the night before she had gone to some man's house. She described in graphic detail how he eagerly dragged off his clothes and begged her to tie him up.

Astrid shrugged. "Well, if that's what you want, buster, you're paying."

She did a good job of roping the man, wrists and ankles, to the bed.

"Now, get a knife and cut me, cut me," he begged.

"Hey, man, I'm not doing that sort of weird stuff. No ways."

"C'mon, lady, just do it. I'm paying. Cut me."

Astrid stood watching him writhe and beg then she picked up his clothes, went through the pockets, took his wallet, helped herself to her fee and a little bit more for "danger pay" and left the man, still tied and pleading to be "cut".

Astrid taught me that it's not life out there on the streets, it's only survival. These girls had been sucked into a very sordid world. Each one of us has the ability to make choices in life, but these girls had not yet come to the point where they understood that. When they did it was usually too late.

"There is no bond between us girls," Astrid once told me. "It's dog eat dog out here on the streets. You'll see, the day I die they'll steal the clothes off my body."

"Aw, c'mon, Astrid, they wouldn't do that," I scoffed.

When we found her some months later she was completely naked. The other prostitutes had stolen everything off her dead body.

Most of the girls were on drugs, their guilt and physical pain so great that drugging was the only way they could do what they had to in order to survive. They started with dagga and then progressed, or should I say, declined, into smoking dagga mixed with Mandrax or "buttons". When the buzz was no longer strong they moved onto Wellconal or "pinks". Drug dealers were always able to buy prescriptions off crooked and greedy local doctors, or the girls would get a prescription from a doctor in exchange for favours. There was never a shortage of Wellconal on the streets of Hillbrow.

These girls didn't live very long. Often it was not the drug itself that was the cause of death, but the movement of a thrombosis that had developed in the groin as a result of "spiking" or injecting drugs. These sad girls were always promising that they would get out, but they never did. Once they were in the culture of prostitution and drugs there seemed to be no way out.

It was in Hillbrow that Laura was found, seven months pregnant and desperately ill. She was brought to The House by a policeman who had taken pity on her. There was nowhere for her to go; the usual homes for single pregnant girls wouldn't touch her as she was both a prostitute and a drug addict. She had gone beyond the primary stage of dagga and was getting someone to "spike" her in the groin.

I got to know her when she came into The House to buy her "schticks" or syringes for spiking. She was twenty and had been on the streets since the age of fifteen. She was a beautiful, vibrant girl from a stern Portuguese or Lebanese family and claimed that she had run away from home after her father had abused her. Perhaps that was why I felt a particular emotional bond with her and longed to play a meaningful role in her life. When she fell pregnant she phoned her parents begging them to take her back, to give her another chance, but they refused.

Laura had never had a birthday party and so Mike and I gave her a surprise party when she turned 21. I remember her sitting in our lounge with the family and in between eating chocolate cake and licking icing off her fingers she had a serious chat with Bernadette and Robyn.

"You guys, look at me. You don't want to land up like I have, on the streets. Don't screw up your lives. You got good parents. Listen to them, love them. Don't ever do what I've done." Bernie and Robyn nodded seriously and promised Laura that they would do as she told them.

Then Laura had her baby and she called him Joshua. She wanted me to look after him. "Debbie, you'll be a good mother for Josh. Just take care of him till I get myself sorted out."

"You've got to get off the drugs, Laura. For Josh's sake."

"Sure, sure. I will. I promise."

Only a week after Josh's birth Laura hit the streets again. She was back into the escort agencies and massage parlours and the clubs in Sandton where all the really perverted "swinging" sex takes place. Then the Welfare people stepped in and put Josh in an official foster home.

I went to her to tell her about Josh. She was living in a dirty back room in one of the clubs in Hillbrow.

"Laura, how are you doing?"

"No, Debbie, I'm fine, just fine." Laura was drinking a glass of iced water. I knew that when the girls needed a fix they would always drink a lot of iced water.

"Laura, are you spiking again?"

"No, Debbie, no. I'm clean. Truly."

"Don't kid me," I said. "I've known you too long for you to bluff me."

She went into the bathroom and when she came back one eye had gone totally squint and I knew for sure that she was on a trip.

Then Laura disappeared. I put word out on the streets but nobody seemed to know where she was. Three weeks later I got a call. She had been taken to hospital after overdosing and on the day that she was going to be transferred to a rehabilitation centre she died very suddenly from a thrombosis. Just a few months after her twenty-first birthday and when her son, Josh, was three months old.

Her body was in the State Mortuary in Pretoria and I was asked to go and identify her. They took me through the back, past all the refrigerators, and there was Laura. I looked down at her. Dear God, it could have been me. It could so easily have been me. She had no covering, she was just lying there, her lovely dark hair a tangled mess around her face, one eye completely squint. I bent over her.

"Yes, Laura," I said, "I can see you've been spiking again, you little bugger."

The mortuary attendant looked at me strangely.

"Why hasn't she got a sheet over her?"

"Ag, lady, she's only a prostitute."

I grabbed hold of his white coat: "You listen to me. She's a human being and she deserves to be treated with dignity. You go now and fetch a sheet and cover her decently."

The funeral parlour people promised that they would "make her look nice" even though she was to have a pauper's funeral. When I went to fetch her ashes I found that her family had been along and collected them. So perhaps in her death they were touched by compassion or guilt although it was too late for Laura and for her little boy, Josh.

These girls are all somebody's children. They all had families they had left and one of the most difficult parts of my job was to counsel the parents. Often we would get a frantic phone call from a grieving mother or father begging us to try to get their daughter to go back home. It was difficult for us to convince the parents that the choice was their daughter's and we could no more than "advise" her. Even those girls from severely dysfunctional homes had left behind one mourning parent, usually a mother.

I learned a lot from the girls on the streets. I had got very close to Astrid and to Laura. I thought I could "make it right" for them by offering them something better. I offered them the possibility of making choices. Looking back, I think that I saw myself as a Ruth in their lives. I hoped that they would grow to love and honour me in the way I loved and honoured Ruth. If I could be the same inspiring example, perhaps one day somewhere down the line they would look back and see me as somebody special who had made a difference. I knew then, as I know now, that there is something in me that is a beacon to those without hope. When I worked in the streets of Hillbrow I had not the insight into myself to work without asking anything in return. I was in too much pain, too needy. Now I know better and as a result I believe my counselling is more balanced and detached. But then it was different. Without realising it, I was heading for a breakdown of monumental proportions.

Most of these girls were rape and childhood abuse victims and I believe that's what bound us together. They were not prostitutes and I a homely housewife. We were all women who had been abused.

These girls simmered with aggression and anger as I did. Most had left home believing that they could make it on their own, and they hadn't. So the anger was turned in towards themselves and was very destructive. I could see it in them but I only recognised it in myself much later. For them every day was a new day. They forgot about the night before, the steamers they had had, the brutality and pain they had had to endure and the drugs they had taken. Today was going to be the day when everything came right for them. A new start, today. By night they knew they hadn't made it, weren't strong enough to get out. They were victims by choice even though they couldn't recognise their part in that choice.

It is sad that society judges and condemns these girls without seeing that there are two sides to their stories. It was all summed up for me by Astrid.

"You know, Debbie, if it wasn't for the steamers we wouldn't have a job."

Chapter 17

I am still in the process of healing and this has taken me on three distinct paths. One was the very vital path of therapy. I could not have progressed without a caring professional like Emma to talk to. Another path was my decision to cooperate in the writing of this book, which was another important part of healing. The third way in which I dealt with my process was to help others who had suffered and were still suffering in the way I had. This was my way, yours will be unique to you.

When I was actively involved in Childline I enjoyed counselling children who had, like me, been sexually, physically and mentally abused. Before I was raped I was able to deal with these children but afterwards I could no longer handle what was happening to them. While I was able to look at my own abuse as someone else's story and believed I was not deeply emotionally affected by it I was able to work with the children. But when my emotional defences were torn away and I had to face my own childhood, it seemed as if each little face was my own and I could no longer face them until I had dealt with my own pain. Sadly I haven't been able to help the children again.

I have had occasion to counsel people who had been bereaved and it became important to me to know how the different religious groups see death. I went to a funeral parlour and they allowed me to do a course in embalming. I learnt that each religion has a different process and different rules pertaining to death and this knowledge helped me tremendously whenever I counselled someone who had lost a loved one. When I saw grieving parents who were worrying about their dead son being "cold" in the mortuary or who wondered how he would be treated at the funeral parlour, I was able to tell them what was going to happen.

It is vitally important for me that when I counsel someone, I know what I am talking about. This has been a driving force in my life. I had been interested in the prison system since a very young child. Once when we were still living in Great Britain Street my father had tried to commit suicide. He had parked his car near the Vaal Dam and fixed a hose pipe to the exhaust and through the window. The local police found him in time and they put him in a cell in the Vereeniging Police Station. Granny May, with me in tow, went down to Vereeniging to bring him back to Johannesburg. I can remember how badly I wanted to go into the cell where my daddy had been. I wanted to know where he had slept and how he had been treated. Even then it was important for me to see how the system worked and what it did to people who were caught up in its folds. What did it look like? What did it feel like for my daddy? If I felt what he felt, smelt the disinfectant with the smell of urine just beneath the surface, if I sat on the bed where he had sat, then maybe I would be able to understand him and maybe even help him.

In Hillbrow when I worked with the girls on the streets I would often hear them talking about going to "Sun City" for the weekend. In my naivety I asked them who took them, did they enjoy the floor shows and did they have a shot at the "one-armed bandits". They laughed and explained that in the street jargon "Sun City" was Diepkloof Prison, just south of Johannesburg. My curiosity was aroused and I went and investigated for myself, learning in the process how the prostitutes were treated when they landed up in the cells. I wouldn't have been taken seriously by the girls unless I had experienced at least a part of their lives.

Once I asked one of the girls why she didn't go into rehabilitation.

"I'll tell you why, Debbie," she said. "I go into rehab and I say to the psychiatrist: `so, you want me to bring you a button?' and he looks down at his shirt buttons and says: `I don't need a button, why you want to bring me a button?' What's the point of talking to these guys when they haven't even made the effort to know our world? They don't know what my world's about, so they can't help me."

There were times when I counselled mothers whose boys were in prison. Other counsellors offered a placebo: "I'm sure he'll be all right. Don't worry," they would say. That wasn't good enough for me. How could I know if it was true? I had to find out.

Speaking to prisoners was a very good experience as I was, for the first time, dealing with the perpetrators and not the victims. I found that prison today is no longer merely a place of incarceration but a place where rehabilitation can take place. I wish someone had offered that to my father. The other side of prison work is to counsel the families of prisoners. These people are also victims, but they are the forgotten ones. In the flurry of the court case and our obvious sympathy with the victim of the crime we often forget that members of the criminal's family have become his victims too. It took a prisoner to tell me that. A boy who does something wrong and lands up in prison has a mother who carries an enormous amount of guilt. What was it in her upbringing of that child that sent him off the rails? The wife of a rapist may have the guilt of wondering whether, if she had been more accommodating, perhaps he wouldn't have done such a terrible thing.

Working with victims can be very draining but I found that working with prisoners was a fulfilling experience. They were giving to me of their vast store of wisdom, knowledge and humour. At last they had someone to listen to them. Often there was no one else: with one psychiatrist for every 5 000 prisoners, not many get the opportunity of having someone empathetic to talk to. Nothing is more rewarding than to go and see a prisoner and have him say, "Yes, my mother told me that you'd been to see her. Thank you. It makes it easier to know that there are people like you outside." They are aware that they have turned their families, the ones they love, into victims and caused a lot of suffering and there is a tremendous amount of guilt and self-anger. I joined Life Line Krugersdorp and became an advisor and trainer on the Rape Crisis Team. I also joined POWA (People Opposed to Women Abuse) and other organisations which deal with similar problems. In the work that I did with rape victims I was often horrified by the seemingly callous way in which the police dealt with women who had been severely traumatised. I had been the victim not only of rapists but also of the police, and I wanted to know why this was happening, so I became a police reservist. Only now have I begun to understand what fierce pressure the police have to work under and I can sympathise with these young men and women instead of condemning them. I have also been able to bring to those policemen with whom I have worked a deeper understanding of what a woman has gone through and how caring they must be to lessen her trauma.

I have been counselling women who have been abused, from a small office in the Paardekraal Hospital in Krugersdorp. This has become the heart of my Crisis Support Centre and is the axis of a wheel of compassion stretching out wherever a woman has been abused or raped and is in need of help. My work has been recognised and this year I was awarded the Community Worker of the Year (1995 - 1996) by Rotary Roodepoort Central.

This work was born out of my memory of how lost I felt just after I had been raped. I needed someone there to help me cope with my runaway emotions and my physical pain, with the legal side, with the trauma of examination by the District Surgeon, and there was no one. I don't want any woman to feel so without support.

This Crisis Support Centre will be there, primarily, for the rape victim, and everything will be under one roof. There will be an examination room where a District Surgeon can examine her and which does not have the sterile atmosphere of a hospital. She won't have to walk through a crowded shopping centre in torn clothes to get to his offices or wait in his waiting room subjected to the curious stares of his patients.

This will be a place where she can receive sympathetic counselling from someone who will understand what she's gone through and what her legal options are. It will be a place where the police can come to take her statement or she can give a statement to a police reservist without having to visit the local police station. There will be stocks of clean clothes and a place where she can take a bath and have a cup of coffee.

The Centre will also be available for battered and abused women, and possibly their children, who may have to get out of their home in the middle of the night. There will be a place for them to sleep with the prospect of being taken to another place of safety when they are ready to move.

I want to see support groups for rape, abuse and childhood sexual abuse survivors, with psychiatrists and psychologists leading the groups to wholeness. I would like to offer the facilities to social work, legal and psychology students, to enable them to gain exposure to the kinds of problems they will have to face in the course of their work. The Centre will also benefit from their enthusiasm and their abilities.

I would also like to see this Centre as a place where our young policemen can feel at home. In Johannesburg there are various steakhouses that offer a free hamburger and cup of coffee to policemen — Bimbo's is an example. On the West Rand there is nothing for them. At the moment there is no debriefing of policemen, no one they can talk to about their horrific day-to-day experiences. After a day's work these youngsters are exhausted and deeply stressed. The Police Force offers no post-traumatic stress assistance whatsoever. We need to have a place where these boys can be debriefed. Perhaps our Centre can be used by them as well.

At the moment we are desperately short of professional people, lawyers, doctors, psychologists, who are prepared to give of their time to victims. We need money to finance the Centre, but we need more than money, we need kindness — and at the moment both are in short supply in South Africa. Our society is in total chaos and will probably remain so well into the next century. It will be necessary for each community to look after its own and not rely on an already over-stretched central government system.

I want to be able to say that at our Centre no one in need will ever be turned away.

Chapter 18

There are things in my life that I can't change. I lost my childhood to a sick, irresponsible man and a domineering tyrant of a grandmother. The basic parental lessons of love, kindness, trust and safety were never mine. Instead I was taught fear, betrayal, both physical and mental pain, and guilt. I can't change the fact that as a child I was isolated from normal friendships by my daily degradation and humiliation. I am learning to accept that with serenity. There is much that I can change and each day I find new courage to do that. I have choices and I am learning to use them.

For the moment the important thing is that I have broken the pattern of destructiveness and torment which was inherent in my family and to which other members of my family still adhere. I shall continue to break the mould because that confirms and validates the person I have become. I can't change the world but I can make a difference in my small corner and I can do so by making myself available as a counsellor to people in trauma no matter their gender or their age.

I am also learning to know what I can't change and what I can.

Working with abused women, rape victims and adult survivors of child-hood sexual abuse is one pathway toward healing. It is my way; it doesn't have to be yours. There are many paths and you will find yours in your own time and in the right place.

My suffering was intensified and prolonged by my self-imposed silence and it has taken me many years to realise that it takes two to survive, whether it is you and a loving and sympathetic partner, you and a therapist or you and your God.

Loneliness is an intrinsic part of what an abuse victim has to endure. It feels as if no one out there understands. With the experience of rape and through therapy and subsequent healing I have learned that each person's trauma is unique. Nobody's experience was quite like mine or yours and no one can feel the pain of another.

I sometimes feel that I have been in a coma for twenty-nine years. Yes, I was a little girl for a short while, and then I slipped into a coma when I was six years old and at the age of thirty-five I came out of that coma and into a different world. I've had to learn to adapt to that world. If you are sitting out there saying, "Yes, but it's because of my childhood. I'm like this because of what my father did, or my brother did, or my uncle or my mother ..." Please, it doesn't have to stay that way. We can't go through life laying the blame on other people for who we are. At some stage we have to call a halt to blaming our pain on parental sins and take responsibility for ourselves. We all have the ability and power to change our lives. It's up to each one of us, though not necessarily alone.

There are choices and there are resources. No one has to stay trapped in a destructive situation. I say to anyone who is either in an abusive relationship or is a rape victim or an adult survivor of childhood sexual abuse — IT CAN BE DIFFERENT. You don't have to stay where you are, but part of your healing will more than likely require the sympathetic help of either a lay counsellor like myself or a professional therapist. I need to emphasise that it's not easy to heal in isolation.

It's good for me to see those that I have counselled starting to make choices in their lives, then I know that they are going to win. There is never anything concrete at the end of counselling, no diploma to hang on the wall, no thank you cards or bunches of flowers. Instead it's the knowledge that some woman feels strong enough to go shopping on her own once again. It's the woman who has finally got herself out of an abusive situation and is standing on her own feet. It's the woman who can look in the mirror and say, "Hey, I'm OK". It's the woman who has reached the point where she can draw on her own resources and begins to trust her own insight and instincts.*

Strangely, I don't regret what happened in the past. I am where I am today because of those experiences and I wouldn't be able to do the things I do without the bedrock knowledge and wisdom those experiences gave me.

I am no longer bitter, but I had to go through a severe mental breakdown before I chose to heal and cast that bitterness and hatred aside. I can now feel a great sense of pity for my grandmother, for Basil and for my mother, for in the end they lost and I gained. The only bitterness I still feel is

*... when we use whatever difficulties we have experienced in order to help others, then all our suffering and struggles are raised up and given purpose and dignity even beyond themselves. They are redeemed.
Why me? Why this? Why now?, by Robin Norwood, p. 11.

towards those two young men who raped me and the system that perpetu-
ated and aggravated that rape. That feeling of bitterness indicates to me
that I still have a long road to travel before I am completely healed of the
experience. And yet, even in that there was the seed of something good
because I was able to break out of the extreme control which was unnaturally holding my life together and become a real feeling person who is
learning to be unafraid of emotions.

We all experience good and bad; the secret is to turn those bad things
around and use them as a springboard to something positive. There were
times that each day followed inexorably on the heels of the one before, not
because I wanted it to, I would much rather have died than face a new day.
But today I can honestly say that I look forward to the sunrise, knowing
that each day brings its own share of joy, fulfilment and peace and that I
can deal with situations that may threaten my new-found inner harmony.

There were those who were a radiant example to me, people like Ruth
Nielsen and Bernie Mullen. They gave me hope at a time when all seemed
hopeless and I shall always be grateful for that. There is Mike, who has
loved me through it all and without whose love nothing would have been
possible. There were those whose tormented lives had an incredibly
destructive impact on mine. But even those I can be grateful for today, for
I learnt much about life and about myself from them. While I will always
bear the scars of my experiences, in many ways I am a contented and peaceful woman.

I could not have come this far without the strong belief in a personal God.
For those who are still in pain from their experiences, I urge you not to lose
sight of God, whatever your personal religious belief system happens to be.
Don't lose hope. We usually feel that, in our darkest moments, God has left
us. I know that when my father was at his most vicious I was convinced
that God had not heard my cries. It was only when I read the following
story by an unknown author many years later that I came to understand
the process:

> One night I had a dream. In my dream I was walking along the beach with
> God and across the sky flashed scenes from my life. In each scene I noticed
> two sets of footprints in the sand, one belonged to me and the other to God.
> But I noticed that at times along the path of life there was only one set of
> footprints. I also noticed that it happened at the very lowest and saddest
> moments of my life. This really bothered me and I questioned God about it.
>
> "God, you said that you would walk with me all the way, but I noticed that
> during the most troubled times of my life there was only one set of foot-
> prints. Why did you desert me in those times when I needed you most?"
>
> God replied, "My precious child, I love you and would never, never leave you
> during your times of trial and suffering. When you see only one set of foot-

prints was when I carried you."

My life was that beach, but it was only on looking back that I was able to see the pattern. I should have died many times. I was often in dangerous situations with ruthless people who had little concern for me as a child. If ever there was a candidate for AIDS or venereal disease it was me and yet I never fell ill. I could have fallen pregnant any time from the age of twelve, but I didn't. Was God's hand evident? I believe so and I am awestruck at the possibility that even evil has a divine purpose.*

It has taken me a long time to come to terms with the understanding that our God-given gift of free will may sometimes become twisted and that little children may become the sad victims of someone else's free choice. It was only when I had started the process of healing that I realised that God had been there all along, even though I wasn't aware of his presence. Even now there are times when I doubt whether I can truly trust God and ask him, "Hey, please be with me on this one". But at quiet times when I am alone and have a chance to listen for that inner voice then I realise that there is no way I can function effectively on my own. I have to acknowledge the power within me is the God-power which I use for the benefit of myself and others.

The storms are behind me and the journey forward will hopefully be one filled with favourable winds and sunny skies.

I made it and you can too.

---

*... just as Prime Creator is in light, it is also in so-called evil, knowing that "evil" also has a divine purpose.
Bringers of the dawn, by Barbara Marciniak, p. 110.

Epilogue

Not only does this book unfold the life of a child who was the innocent victim of the passions, frustrations and cruelties of the adults in her life, it also touches on the craven behaviour of those who "knew" or "suspected" that there was something amiss but did nothing. If only there had been just one person with the courage to act on her instincts ...

More importantly, however, it is the story of a very brave and unique young woman who chose not to cling to the grim details of her youth and use those awful episodes as an excuse to harm others or to continue the harm to herself. Instead she chose to heal from the wounds of the past and, in healing, has become an example to all whose lives she touches.

Debbie Neville's story, however, raises as many questions as it tries to answer. We are forced to wonder why some children are born into addictive and dysfunctional families in the first place. Is there a kind of "hiccup", a weakness in God's plan, that allows a child like Debbie to become a helpless victim? Or was there, prior to her birth, a "plan" in which her spiritual growth would be accelerated by certain experiences? If so, what part did Basil Nicholls play in that plan? It is obvious that through his actions he played a vital role in Debbie's spiritual growth — for, without the painful experiences of her childhood, she could not have reached the level of compassion, spiritual awareness and deep understanding which she now possesses. Did Basil, as suggested by the author and therapist Robin Norwood, offer up this lifetime as a gesture of love and service to become the catalyst for his daughter's spiritual progress?* And, if this was the case,

---

*A daughter who incarnates with a mission to advance understanding of the dynamics of violence may require a brutal father to provide her with the necessary field of experience ... she use[s] his treatment of her as the springboard to her own deeper understanding and healing ... both she and her father have, together, become instruments of healing.
Why me? Why this? Why now? by Robin Norwood, p. 155.

by what standards do we judge him? Norwood presumes reincarnation and the argument for or against this concept is beyond the scope of this book. There is, however, a beautifully poignant reference to reincarnation in Proverbs 8: 22-30 which possibly supports Norwood's theory:

> *The Lord possessed me in the beginning of his way,*
> *before his works of old.*

> *I was set up from everlasting, from the beginning,*
> *or ever the earth was.*

> *When there were no depths, I was brought forth; when*
> *there were no fountains abounding with water.*

> *... When he prepared the heavens, I was there ...*

> *Then was I by him, as one brought up with him;*
> *and I was daily his delight ...*

Surely a life as fraught with pain and ugliness as Debbie's is not in the design of a just and loving God. Even taking the gift of free will into account, how can a loving Father/Mother God stand by and watch an innocent being depraved in this way? It makes no sense! But if Debbie "chose" at some level of her immortality, to incarnate under these conditions and for a special purpose then such a life becomes more understandable.*

We are too fallible to understand the mind of the Great Spirit and we can only make puerile assumptions as to his purpose and intent. God is unknowable to us in our present finite form and it would be arrogance on our part even to assume that we can fathom the whole purpose of either our suffering or our joy.

We can only live our lives in the understanding that we are instruments of God, knowing that he does not give us experiences or tasks for which we have not been prepared.

As with each of us, Debbie's healing process has been cyclical. With each spiral of the cycle has come a greater testing which, in turn, has brought about a greater opportunity to learn, to change and to grow. There were times in Debbie's life when she was unable to grab hold of the growth opportunity because it was just too difficult to let go of elements of her experiences which were "safe" or "comfortable" for her, for example the

---

*One wonders why men have so readily accepted a life after death and so largely, in the West, discarded the idea of a life before birth. So many arguments for a one-way mortality seem to me cogent for a two-way life outside the present body.

Dean Inge quoted by Noel Langley in *Edgar Cayce on reincarnation*, p. 278.

fierce control she had over her life and emotions and the lives of those around her. Often we find there is a comfort zone, however disagreeable, from which it is risky to move and Debbie could not progress from the role of controller/manipulator until she was forced to by the terrible event in Port Elizabeth. Also, even though Debbie may not have been aware of it at the time and indeed may not have indulged in it overtly, playing the role of victim absolved her from the hazardous responsibility of her own growth. After the breakdown in Krugersdorp it became apparent that she had no choice but to follow a healing path; the only choice she had was when, not if.

Her first healing spiral began at the age of fifteen in Vanderbijlpark when she found the courage to say — *No! Enough! No more!* It was at that moment that she used her God-gift of free will and stopped being the passive victim of her father's predatory nature.

Debbie's marriages brought further opportunities to change and grow, as did the birth of her three children (no child comes into the world without bringing its own power to heal). Debbie made only limited use of these opportunities simply because at the time she was not ready to address the deepest and most painful part of her own healing process — the healing of her inner child.

Unknowingly Debbie slowed down the healing process by being "in control" of her memories and by manipulating her environment so that she did not have to deal with her past. She was also unable, at that stage, to confront the worst in her own nature, to recognise that by being "in control" she was following the example of the other malevolent character in her life, her grandmother. It would have taken more wisdom than Debbie had at the time to accept those parts of herself for which May, the controlling, manipulative female, was her mirror image.

I believe that we are all born with a spiritual blueprint of which we are co-author with God and his hierarchy. This blueprint is the basic design of what we hope to achieve in a particular lifetime in order to be absorbed finally back into the Great Spirit from which we emanate. The details of all previous experiences are mercifully blanked from our senses, as are the previous lifetime's hopes, failures, successes and tragedies. Unless we come to an understanding and acceptance of this it is difficult to accept that there may be a self-imposed purpose behind our individual suffering and pain as well as our joy and happiness. It would not be unexpected if Debbie did not wish to confront the possibility that she may have chosen to attend to this particular area of learning in this lifetime, with all its concomitant anguish and loss. It may not even be important for her at this time.

Perhaps the most important lesson for her at this stage of her spiritual development is the understanding that all her most significant relationships, both good and bad, have had one purpose and one purpose only, and that is to lead her towards the Light. If there is any validity in such thoughts then we need to acknowledge that if Basil Nicholls was her nemesis then so too was he her path to salvation.

The opportunity for healing comes to us very often after a crisis, and it seems that the greater the crisis the greater the possibility of healing — if we choose to heal. Suffering becomes a catalyst for change if we can but recognise its potential and find the courage to work through our pain and thereby redeem it and give it purpose.

Debbie has come to understand that she is an integral part of the cosmos, and that when she works at her healing process she does so for the entire body of humanity. Just as when she was injured by her father, by May and by the others all humanity experienced her pain and was diminished by it. On a cosmic level the hurting of one hurts all and the healing of one heals all.

For the moment the storms are over. Debbie will have other crises, other opportunities for spirals of healing but, for the present, she stands at the point where her past begins to fall into some kind of perspective and she can allow herself to let go, where she is beginning to have a gentle understanding of the purpose of her individual existence and her place in the universe.

This is her true healing.

Jenny Harrison

BIBLIOGRAPHY

There are many books that can be useful to survivors and to professionals. Gerald Jampolsky and Leo Buscaglia have written much that can assist in healing and there are others. The one book that I found the most helpful was *The courage to heal* by Ellen Bass and Laura Davis.

Bass, Ellen and Davis, Laura, *The courage to heal*, Harper & Row, New York, 1988.

Feste, Catherine, *The physician within*, Diabetes Center, Minneapolis, 1987.

Hagens, Kathryn B and Case, Joyce, *When your child has been molested*, Lexington Books, New York, 1988.

Langley, Noel, *Edgar Cayce on reincarnation*, Paperback Library, Coronet Corp, New York, 1967.

Lewis, Sharon, *Dealing with rape*, Sached Books, Johannesburg, 1994.

Maltz, Wendy, *The sexual healing journey*, Harper Perennial, New York, 1992.

Marciniak, Barbara, *Bringers of the dawn*, Bear & Company Publishing, Sante Fe, New Mexico, 1992.

Martin, Laura C, *A life without fear*, Rutledge Hill Press, Nashville, Tennessee, 1992.

Norwood, Robin, *Why me? Why this? Why now?*, Arrow Books, Random House, London, 1994.

Peck, M Scott, *People of the lie*, Century Hutchinson Ltd, London, 1983.

Robertson, Grant, *Sexual abuse of children in South Africa*, Unibook Publishers, Hammanskraal, 1989.

Sanford, Paula, *Healing victims of sexual abuse*, Victory House Publishers, Tulsa, Oklahoma, 1988.

Seymour jnr, Whitney North, *Making a difference*, William Morrow & Co Inc, New York, 1984.

Tate, Tim, *Child pornography, an investigation*, Metheun, London, 1990.

REFERRALS

If you or anyone you know is in trouble, here are a few telephone numbers which may be useful:

- POWA (People Against Women Abuse) —
  Johannesburg, tel: (011) 642-4345

- Childline — tel: 0800-055-555

- Safeline (part of Childline) — Cape Town, tel: (021) 638-1155

- Rape Crisis — Durban, tel: (031) 23-0904;
  Port Elizabeth, tel: (041) 57-1997

- Vista Rape Crisis — Pretoria, tel: (012) 323-1020;
  Cape Town, tel: (021) 47-9762; Port Elizabeth, tel: (041) 801- 0210;
  Pietermaritzburg, tel: (0331) 45-6297; Krugersdorp,
  tel: (011) 339-4481 (code 6128); Hillbrow, tel: (011) 886-8745

- Life Line — look in your telephone directory for your local branch

- South African Police Child Protection Unit — Johannesburg,
  tel: (011) 403-3413; Pretoria, tel: (012) 329-6872

- Crisis Support Centre — Krugersdorp (Paardekraal Hospital),
  tel: (083) 227-9555 or (011) 339-4481 (code 6128)